MznLnx

Missing Links Exam Preps

Exam Prep for

Marketing Research: Methodological Foundations

Churchill & Iacobucci, 9th Edition

The MznLnx Exam Prep is your link from the texbook and lecture to your exams.
The MznLnx Exam Preps are unauthorized and comprehensive reviews of your textbooks.

All material provided by MznLnx and Rico Publications (c) 2010
Textbook publishers and textbook authors do not particpate in or contribute to these reviews.

MznLnx

Rico
Publications

Exam Prep for Marketing Research: Methodological Foundations
9th Edition
Churchill & Iacobucci

Publisher: Raymond Houge
Assistant Editor: Michael Rouger
Text and Cover Designer: Lisa Buckner
Marketing Manager: Sara Swagger
Project Manager, Editorial Production: Jerry Emerson
Art Director: Vernon Lowerui

Product Manager: Dave Mason
Editorial Assitant: Rachel Guzmanji
Pedagogy: Debra Long
Cover Image: Jim Reed/Getty Images
Text and Cover Printer: City Printing, Inc.
Compositor: Media Mix, Inc.

(c) 2010 Rico Publications
ALL RIGHTS RESERVED. No part of this work covered by the copyright may be reproduced or used in any form or by an means--graphic, electronic, or mechanical, including photocopying, recording, taping, Web distribution, information storage, and retrieval systems, or in any other manner--without the written permission of the publisher.

For more information about our products, contact us at:
Dave.Mason@RicoPublications.com

For permission to use material from this text or product, submit a request online to:
Dave.Mason@RicoPublications.com

Printed in the United States
ISBN:

Contents

CHAPTER 1
Marketing Research: It`s Everywhere! — 1

CHAPTER 2
Alternative Approaches to Marketing Intelligence — 8

CHAPTER 3
The Research Process and Problem Formulation — 13

CHAPTER 4
Research Design, Exploratory Research, and Qualitative Data — 21

CHAPTER 5
Descriptive Research — 27

CHAPTER 6
Causal Designs — 29

CHAPTER 7
Data Collection: Secondary Data — 39

CHAPTER 8
Data Collection: Primary Data — 48

CHAPTER 9
Questionnaires and Data-Collection Forms — 56

CHAPTER 10
Attitude Measurement — 61

CHAPTER 11
Sampling Procedures — 67

CHAPTER 12
Determining Sample Size — 72

CHAPTER 13
Collecting the Data: Field Procedures and Nonsampling Errors — 75

CHAPTER 14
Preprocessing the Data, and Doing Cross-Tabs — 80

CHAPTER 15
Data Analysis—Basic Questions — 84

CHAPTER 16
Are My Groups the Same or Different? — 88

CHAPTER 17
Are These Variables Related? — 91

CHAPTER 18
Multivariate Data Analysis — 96

CHAPTER 19
The Research Report — 103

ANSWER KEY — 127

TO THE STUDENT

COMPREHENSIVE

The *MznLnx* Exam Prep series is designed to help you pass your exams. Editors at MznLnx review your textbooks and then prepare these practice exams to help you master the textbook material. Unlike study guides, workbooks, and practice tests provided by the texbook publisher and textbook authors, *MznLnx* gives you **all** of the material in each chapter in exam form, not just samples, so you can be sure to nail your exam.

MECHANICAL

The MznLnx Exam Prep series creates exams that will help you learn the subject matter as well as test you on your understanding. Each question is designed to help you master the concept. Just working through the exams, you gain an understanding of the subject--its a simple mechanical process that produces success.

INTEGRATED STUDY GUIDE AND REVIEW

MznLnx is not just a set of exams designed to test you, its also a comprehensive review of the subject content. Each exam question is also a review of the concept, making sure that you will get the answer correct without having to go to other sources of material. You learn as you go! Its the easiest way to pass an exam.

HUMOR

Studying can be tedious and dry. MznLnx's instructional design includes moderate humor within the exam questions on occassion, to break the tedium and revitalize the brain

Chapter 1. Marketing Research: It`s Everywhere!

1. The _____ is a professional association for marketers. As of 2008 it had approximately 40,000 members. There are collegiate chapters on 250 campuses.
   a. ADTECH
   b. ACNielsen
   c. AMAX
   d. American Marketing Association

2. _____ is defined by the American _____ Association as the activity, set of institutions, and processes for creating, communicating, delivering, and exchanging offerings that have value for customers, clients, partners, and society at large. The term developed from the original meaning which referred literally to going to market, as in shopping, or going to a market to sell goods or services.

   _____ practice tends to be seen as a creative industry, which includes advertising, distribution and selling.

   a. Marketing myopia
   b. Customer acquisition management
   c. Product naming
   d. Marketing

3. Consumer market research is a form of applied sociology that concentrates on understanding the behaviours, whims and preferences, of consumers in a market-based economy, and aims to understand the effects and comparative success of marketing campaigns. The field of consumer _____ as a statistical science was pioneered by Arthur Nielsen with the founding of the ACNielsen Company in 1923 .

   Thus _____ is the systematic and objective identification, collection, analysis, and dissemination of information for the purpose of assisting management in decision making related to the identification and solution of problems and opportunities in marketing.

   a. Focus group
   b. Marketing research process
   c. Logit analysis
   d. Marketing research

4. The term _____ is primarily used by mass media to describe any form of synchronous conferencing, occasionally even asynchronous conferencing. The term can thus mean any technology ranging from real-time online chat over instant messaging and online forums to fully immersive graphical social environments.

   Online chat is a way of communicating by sending text messages to people in the same chat-room in real-time.

a. 6-3-5 Brainwriting
b. Chat room
c. Power III
d. 180SearchAssistant

5. An _____ is one type of focus group, and is a sub-set of online research methods.

A moderator invites prescreened, qualified respondents who represent the target of interest to log on to conferencing software at a pre-arranged time and to take part in an _____. Some researchers will offer incentives for participating but this raises a number of ethical questions.

a. Intangibility
b. Engagement
c. Automated surveys
d. Online focus group

6. A _____ is a form of qualitative research in which a group of people are asked about their attitude towards a product, service, concept, advertisement, idea, or packaging. Questions are asked in an interactive group setting where participants are free to talk with other group members.

Ernest Dichter originated the idea of having a 'group therapy' for products and this process is what became known as a _____.

a. Marketing research process
b. Focus group
c. Cross tabulation
d. Logit analysis

7. _____ refer to a collection of facts usually collected as the result of experience, observation or experiment or a set of premises. This may consist of numbers, words particularly as measurements or observations of a set of variables. _____ are often viewed as a lowest level of abstraction from which information and knowledge are derived.

a. Pearson product-moment correlation coefficient
b. Data
c. Sample size
d. Mean

Chapter 1. Marketing Research: It's Everywhere!

8. _____ is a business discipline which is focused on the practical application of marketing techniques and the management of a firm's marketing resources and activities. Marketing managers are often responsible for influencing the level, timing, and composition of customer demand accepted definition of the term. In part, this is because the role of a marketing manager can vary significantly based on a business' size, corporate culture, and industry context.
   a. Performance-based advertising
   b. Door-to-door
   c. Marketing management
   d. Business structure

9. _____ is the collection and management of information from one or more sources and the distribution of that information to one or more audiences. This sometimes involves those who have a stake in, or a right to that information. Management means the organization of and control over the structure, processing and delivery of information.
   a. ACNielsen
   b. AMAX
   c. Information management
   d. ADTECH

10. A _____ captures, stores, analyzes, manages, and presents data that is linked to location.

In the strictest sense, the term describes any information system that integrates, stores, edits, analyzes, shares, and displays geographic information. In a more generic sense, _____ applications are tools that allow users to create interactive queries (user created searches), analyze spatial information, edit data, maps, and present the results of all these operations.

   a. 6-3-5 Brainwriting
   b. Geographic information system
   c. 180SearchAssistant
   d. Power III

11. _____ refers to marketing strategies applied directly to a specific consumer.

Having the knowledge on the consumer preferences, there are suggested personalized products and promotions to each consumer.

The _____ is based in four main steps in order to fulfill its goals: Those stages are identify, differentiate, interact, and customize.

a. AMAX
b. ADTECH
c. ACNielsen
d. One-to-one marketing

12. _____ in its literal sense is the process of transformation of local or regional phenomena into global ones. It can be described as a process by which the people of the world are unified into a single society and function together.

This process is a combination of economic, technological, sociocultural and political forces.

a. Globalization
b. 180SearchAssistant
c. Power III
d. 6-3-5 Brainwriting

13. _____ is a measure of the strength of a brand, product, service relative to competitive offerings. There is often a geographic element to the competitive landscape. In defining _____, you must see to what extent a product, brand, or firm controls a product category in a given geographic area.
a. Market dominance
b. Market system
c. Discretionary spending
d. Productivity

14. _____ is the practice of individuals including commercial businesses, governments and institutions, facilitating the sale of their products or services to other companies or organizations that in turn resell them, use them as components in products or services they offer _____ is also called business-to-_____ for short. (Note that while marketing to government entities shares some of the same dynamics of organizational marketing, B2G Marketing is meaningfully different.)
a. Mass marketing
b. Disruptive technology
c. Business marketing
d. Law of disruption

15. _____ is a global marketing research firm, with worldwide headquarters in New York City. Regional headquarters for North America are located in Schaumburg, IL. As of 2008, its the part of The Nielsen Company.

a. ACNielsen
b. Alloy Entertainment
c. E-Detailing
d. InfoNU

16. Electronic commerce, commonly known as _____ or eCommerce, consists of the buying and selling of products or services over electronic systems such as the Internet and other computer networks. The amount of trade conducted electronically has grown extraordinarily with wide-spread Internet usage. A wide variety of commerce is conducted in this way, spurring and drawing on innovations in electronic funds transfer, supply chain management, Internet marketing, online transaction processing, electronic data interchange (EDI), inventory management systems, and automated data collection systems.
a. ADTECH
b. AMAX
c. E-commerce
d. ACNielsen

17. Human beings are also considered to be _____ because they have the ability to change raw materials into valuable _____. The term Human _____ can also be defined as the skills, energies, talents, abilities and knowledge that are used for the production of goods or the rendering of services. While taking into account human beings as _____, the following things have to be kept in mind:

- The size of the population
- The capabilities of the individuals in that population

Many _____ cannot be consumed in their original form. They have to be processed in order to change them into more usable commodities.

a. Resources
b. 180SearchAssistant
c. 6-3-5 Brainwriting
d. Power III

18. '_____' is a class of statistical techniques that can be applied to data that exhibit 'natural' groupings. _____ sorts through the raw data and groups them into clusters. A cluster is a group of relatively homogeneous cases or observations.

a. 180SearchAssistant
b. Structure mining
c. Power III
d. Cluster analysis

19. _____ is an advertisement in which a particular product specifically mentions a competitor by name for the express purpose of showing why the competitor is inferior to the product naming it.

This should not be confused with parody advertisements, where a fictional product is being advertised for the purpose of poking fun at the particular advertisement, nor should it be confused with the use of a coined brand name for the purpose of comparing the product without actually naming an actual competitor. ('Wikipedia tastes better and is less filling than the Encyclopedia Galactica.')

In the 1980s, during what has been referred to as the cola wars, soft-drink manufacturer Pepsi ran a series of advertisements where people, caught on hidden camera, in a blind taste test, chose Pepsi over rival Coca-Cola.

a. GL-70
b. Cost per conversion
c. Heavy-up
d. Comparative advertising

20. A _____ is a collection of symbols, experiences and associations connected with a product, a service, a person or any other artifact or entity.

_____s have become increasingly important components of culture and the economy, now being described as 'cultural accessories and personal philosophies'.

Some people distinguish the psychological aspect of a _____ from the experiential aspect.

a. Brand equity
b. Brand
c. Store brand
d. Brandable software

21. _____ is a contract between two parties, one being the employer and the other being the employee. An employee may be defined as: 'A person in the service of another under any contract of hire, express or implied, oral or written, where the employer has the power or right to control and direct the employee in the material details of how the work is to be performed.' Black's Law Dictionary page 471 (5th ed. 1979.)

a. Employment
b. ADTECH
c. AMAX
d. ACNielsen

Chapter 2. Alternative Approaches to Marketing Intelligence

1. _____ is defined by the American _____ Association as the activity, set of institutions, and processes for creating, communicating, delivering, and exchanging offerings that have value for customers, clients, partners, and society at large. The term developed from the original meaning which referred literally to going to market, as in shopping, or going to a market to sell goods or services.

_____ practice tends to be seen as a creative industry, which includes advertising, distribution and selling.

   a. Marketing myopia
   b. Product naming
   c. Customer acquisition management
   d. Marketing

2. _____ refer to a collection of facts usually collected as the result of experience, observation or experiment or a set of premises. This may consist of numbers, words particularly as measurements or observations of a set of variables. _____ are often viewed as a lowest level of abstraction from which information and knowledge are derived.

   a. Sample size
   b. Mean
   c. Pearson product-moment correlation coefficient
   d. Data

3. _____ is an advertisement in which a particular product specifically mentions a competitor by name for the express purpose of showing why the competitor is inferior to the product naming it.

This should not be confused with parody advertisements, where a fictional product is being advertised for the purpose of poking fun at the particular advertisement, nor should it be confused with the use of a coined brand name for the purpose of comparing the product without actually naming an actual competitor. ('Wikipedia tastes better and is less filling than the Encyclopedia Galactica.')

In the 1980s, during what has been referred to as the cola wars, soft-drink manufacturer Pepsi ran a series of advertisements where people, caught on hidden camera, in a blind taste test, chose Pepsi over rival Coca-Cola.

   a. Comparative advertising
   b. Heavy-up
   c. Cost per conversion
   d. GL-70

4. An _____ is the manufacturing of a good or service within a category. Although _____ is a broad term for any kind of economic production, in economics and urban planning _____ is a synonym for the secondary sector, which is a type of economic activity involved in the manufacturing of raw materials into goods and products.

Chapter 2. Alternative Approaches to Marketing Intelligence

There are four key industrial economic sectors: the primary sector, largely raw material extraction industries such as mining and farming; the secondary sector, involving refining, construction, and manufacturing; the tertiary sector, which deals with services (such as law and medicine) and distribution of manufactured goods; and the quaternary sector, a relatively new type of knowledge _____ focusing on technological research, design and development such as computer programming, and biochemistry.

a. Industry
b. ACNielsen
c. AMAX
d. ADTECH

5. _____ is the process of extracting hidden patterns from data. As more data is gathered, with the amount of data doubling every three years, _____ is becoming an increasingly important tool to transform this data into information. It is commonly used in a wide range of profiling practices, such as marketing, surveillance, fraud detection and scientific discovery.
a. Power III
b. Structure mining
c. 180SearchAssistant
d. Data mining

6. A _____ is a structured collection of records or data that is stored in a computer system. The structure is achieved by organizing the data according to a _____ model. The model in most common use today is the relational model.
a. 6-3-5 Brainwriting
b. Power III
c. Database
d. 180SearchAssistant

7. _____ is that part of statistical practice concerned with the selection of individual observations intended to yield some knowledge about a population of concern, especially for the purposes of statistical inference. Each observation measures one or more properties (weight, location, etc.) of an observable entity enumerated to distinguish objects or individuals.
a. AStore
b. Richard Buckminster 'Bucky' Fuller
c. Sampling
d. Sports Marketing Group

Chapter 2. Alternative Approaches to Marketing Intelligence

8. _____ is the imitation of some real thing, state of affairs, or process. The act of simulating something generally entails representing certain key characteristics or behaviors of a selected physical or abstract system.

_____ is used in many contexts, including the modeling of natural systems or human systems in order to gain insight into their functioning.

a. 180SearchAssistant
b. 6-3-5 Brainwriting
c. Power III
d. Simulation

9. _____ is a form of direct marketing using databases of customers or potential customers to generate personalized communications in order to promote a product or service for marketing purposes. The method of communication can be any addressable medium, as in direct marketing.

The distinction between direct and _____ stems primarily from the attention paid to the analysis of data.

a. Power III
b. Direct marketing
c. Direct Marketing Associations
d. Database marketing

10. _____ is a sub-discipline and type of marketing. There are two main definitional characteristics which distinguish it from other types of marketing. The first is that it attempts to send its messages directly to consumers, without the use of intervening media.

a. Power III
b. Direct marketing
c. Direct Marketing Associations
d. Database marketing

11. Consumer market research is a form of applied sociology that concentrates on understanding the behaviours, whims and preferences, of consumers in a market-based economy, and aims to understand the effects and comparative success of marketing campaigns. The field of consumer _____ as a statistical science was pioneered by Arthur Nielsen with the founding of the ACNielsen Company in 1923.

Thus _____ is the systematic and objective identification, collection, analysis, and dissemination of information for the purpose of assisting management in decision making related to the identification and solution of problems and opportunities in marketing.

a. Marketing research
b. Focus group
c. Logit analysis
d. Marketing research process

12. _____ constitute a class of computer-based information systems including knowledge-based systems that support decision-making activities.

_____ are a specific class of computerized information system that supports business and organizational decision-making activities. A properly-designed _____ is an interactive software-based system intended to help decision makers compile useful information from raw data, documents, personal knowledge, and/or business models to identify and solve problems and make decisions.

a. 6-3-5 Brainwriting
b. Power III
c. Decision support systems
d. 180SearchAssistant

13. A _____ is a commercial building for storage of goods. _____s are used by manufacturers, importers, exporters, wholesalers, transport businesses, customs, etc. They are usually large plain buildings in industrial areas of cities and towns.
a. Warehouse
b. 180SearchAssistant
c. 6-3-5 Brainwriting
d. Power III

14. _____s are structured marketing efforts that reward, and therefore encourage, loyal buying behaviour -- behaviour which is potentially of benefit to the firm.

In marketing generally and in retailing more specifically, a loyalty card, rewards card, points card, advantage card, or club card is a plastic or paper card, visually similar to a credit card or debit card, that identifies the card holder as a member in a _____. Loyalty cards are a system of the loyalty business model.

a. Loyalty program
b. Power III
c. 6-3-5 Brainwriting
d. 180SearchAssistant

Chapter 2. Alternative Approaches to Marketing Intelligence

15. _____, also referred to as i-marketing, web marketing, online marketing is the marketing of products or services over the Internet.

The Internet has brought many unique benefits to marketing, one of which being lower costs for the distribution of information and media to a global audience. The interactive nature of _____, both in terms of providing instant response and eliciting responses, is a unique quality of the medium.

 a. AMAX
 b. ADTECH
 c. Internet marketing
 d. ACNielsen

16. The _____ is a very large set of interlinked hypertext documents accessed via the Internet. With a Web browser, one can view Web pages that may contain text, images, videos, and other multimedia and navigate between them using hyperlinks. Using concepts from earlier hypertext systems, the _____ was begun in 1992 by the English physicist Sir Tim Berners-Lee, now the Director of the _____ Consortium, and Robert Cailliau, a Belgian computer scientist, while both were working at CERN in Geneva, Switzerland.
 a. Power III
 b. World Wide Web
 c. 6-3-5 Brainwriting
 d. 180SearchAssistant

17. _____ , according to Cornish, 'the process of acquiring and analyzing information in order to understand the market (both existing and potential customers); to determine the current and future needs and preferences, attitudes and behavior of the market; and to assess changes in the business environment that may affect the size and nature of the market in the future.' ('Product', 1997, p147.)

This figure shows how the interaction between variables from producers, communication channels, and consumers vary the effectiveness of _____ which affects the performance of the sales of a new product. The product is central in a circle because it helps to direct what information is gathered and how.

 a. Market intelligence
 b. Line extension
 c. Brand parity
 d. Co-branding

Chapter 3. The Research Process and Problem Formulation

1. A _____ is a plan of action designed to achieve a particular goal.

   _____ is different from tactics. In military terms, tactics is concerned with the conduct of an engagement while _____ is concerned with how different engagements are linked.

   a. Power III
   b. 6-3-5 Brainwriting
   c. 180SearchAssistant
   d. Strategy

2. _____ is a type of research conducted because a problem has not been clearly defined. _____ helps determine the best research design, data collection method and selection of subjects. Given its fundamental nature, _____ often concludes that a perceived problem does not actually exist.
   a. ACNielsen
   b. Exploratory research
   c. IDDEA
   d. Intent scale translation

3. _____ is a way of expressing knowledge or belief that an event will occur or has occurred. In mathematics the concept has been given an exact meaning in _____ theory, that is used extensively in such areas of study as mathematics, statistics, finance, gambling, science, and philosophy to draw conclusions about the likelihood of potential events and the underlying mechanics of complex systems.
   a. Linear regression
   b. Heteroskedastic
   c. Data
   d. Probability

4. A sample is a subject chosen from a population for investigation. A _____ is one chosen by a method involving an unpredictable component. Random sampling can also refer to taking a number of independent observations from the same probability distribution, without involving any real population.
   a. 180SearchAssistant
   b. Random sample
   c. Selection bias
   d. Power III

Chapter 3. The Research Process and Problem Formulation

5. A number of different _____ s are indicated below.

- Randomized controlled trial
    - Double-blind randomized trial
    - Single-blind randomized trial
    - Non-blind trial
- Nonrandomized trial (quasi-experiment)
    - Interrupted time series design (measures on a sample or a series of samples from the same population are obtained several times before and after a manipulated event or a naturally occurring event) - considered a type of quasi-experiment

- Cohort study
    - Prospective cohort
    - Retrospective cohort
    - Time series study
- Case-control study
    - Nested case-control study
- Cross-sectional study
    - Community survey (a type of cross-sectional study)

When choosing a _____, many factors must be taken into account. Different types of studies are subject to different types of bias. For example, recall bias is likely to occur in cross-sectional or case-control studies where subjects are asked to recall exposure to risk factors.

a. Study design
b. Power III
c. Longitudinal studies
d. 180SearchAssistant

6. _____ is that part of statistical practice concerned with the selection of individual observations intended to yield some knowledge about a population of concern, especially for the purposes of statistical inference. Each observation measures one or more properties (weight, location, etc.) of an observable entity enumerated to distinguish objects or individuals.
a. Sports Marketing Group
b. Richard Buckminster 'Bucky' Fuller
c. Sampling
d. AStore

7. In statistics, a simple random sample is a subset of individuals (a sample) chosen from a larger set (a population.) Each individual is chosen randomly and entirely by chance, such that each individual has the same probability of being chosen at any stage during the sampling process, and each subset of k individuals has the same probability of being chosen for the sample as any other subset of k individuals (.) This process and technique is known as _____, and should not be confused with Random Sampling.
   a. Logit analysis
   b. Simple random sampling
   c. Market analysis
   d. Focus group

8. A _____ is a structured collection of records or data that is stored in a computer system. The structure is achieved by organizing the data according to a _____ model. The model in most common use today is the relational model.
   a. Power III
   b. 180SearchAssistant
   c. 6-3-5 Brainwriting
   d. Database

9. The _____ of a statistical sample is the number of observations that constitute it. It is typically denoted n, a positive integer (natural number.)

Typically, all else being equal, a larger _____ leads to increased precision in estimates of various properties of the population.

   a. Heteroskedastic
   b. Data
   c. Frequency distribution
   d. Sample size

10. _____ refer to a collection of facts usually collected as the result of experience, observation or experiment or a set of premises. This may consist of numbers, words particularly as measurements or observations of a set of variables. _____ are often viewed as a lowest level of abstraction from which information and knowledge are derived.
    a. Mean
    b. Pearson product-moment correlation coefficient
    c. Sample size
    d. Data

11. Combining Existing _____ Sources with New Primary Data Sources

Imagine that we could get hold of a good collection of surveys taken in earlier years, such as detailed studies about changes going on in this phase and hopefully additional studies in the years to come. Analyzing this data base over time could give us a good picture of what changes actually have taken place in the orientation of the population and of the extent to which new technical concepts did have an impact on subgroups of the population. Furthermore, data archives can help to prepare studies on change over time by monitoring what questions have been asked in earlier years and alerting principal investigators to important questions which should be repeated in planned research projects.

a. 180SearchAssistant
b. 6-3-5 Brainwriting
c. Secondary data
d. Power III

12. In statistics, analysis of variance (_____) is a collection of statistical models, and their associated procedures, in which the observed variance is partitioned into components due to different explanatory variables. In its simplest form _____ gives a statistical test of whether the means of several groups are all equal, and therefore generalizes Student's two-sample t-test to more than two groups.

There are three conceptual classes of such models:

1. Fixed-effects models assumes that the data came from normal populations which may differ only in their means. (Model 1)
2. Random effects models assume that the data describe a hierarchy of different populations whose differences are constrained by the hierarchy. (Model 2)
3. Mixed-effect models describe situations where both fixed and random effects are present. (Model 3)

In practice, there are several types of _____ depending on the number of treatments and the way they are applied to the subjects in the experiment:

- One-way _____ is used to test for differences among two or more independent groups. Typically, however, the one-way _____ is used to test for differences among at least three groups, since the two-group case can be covered by a T-test (Gossett, 1908.)

a. AMAX
b. ADTECH
c. ANOVA
d. ACNielsen

Chapter 3. The Research Process and Problem Formulation

13. _____s are errors in measurement that lead to measured values being inconsistent when repeated measures of a constant attribute or quantity are taken. The word random indicates that they are inherently unpredictable, and have null expected value, namely, they are scattered about the true value, and tend to have null arithmetic mean when a measurement is repeated several times with the same instrument. All measurements are prone to _____.

   a. Random error
   b. Systematic error
   c. 180SearchAssistant
   d. Power III

14. _____ is defined by the American _____ Association as the activity, set of institutions, and processes for creating, communicating, delivering, and exchanging offerings that have value for customers, clients, partners, and society at large. The term developed from the original meaning which referred literally to going to market, as in shopping, or going to a market to sell goods or services.

   _____ practice tends to be seen as a creative industry, which includes advertising, distribution and selling.

   a. Marketing myopia
   b. Product naming
   c. Marketing
   d. Customer acquisition management

15. Consumer market research is a form of applied sociology that concentrates on understanding the behaviours, whims and preferences, of consumers in a market-based economy, and aims to understand the effects and comparative success of marketing campaigns. The field of consumer _____ as a statistical science was pioneered by Arthur Nielsen with the founding of the ACNielsen Company in 1923 .

   Thus _____ is the systematic and objective identification, collection, analysis, and dissemination of information for the purpose of assisting management in decision making related to the identification and solution of problems and opportunities in marketing.

   a. Logit analysis
   b. Marketing research process
   c. Focus group
   d. Marketing research

16. _____ can be regarded as an outcome of mental processes (cognitive process) leading to the selection of a course of action among several alternatives. Every _____ process produces a final choice. The output can be an action or an opinion of choice.

a. 6-3-5 Brainwriting
b. Decision making
c. Power III
d. 180SearchAssistant

17. _____ is the management of the flow of goods, information and other resources, including energy and people, between the point of origin and the point of consumption in order to meet the requirements of consumers (frequently, and originally, military organizations.) _____ involves the integration of information, transportation, inventory, warehousing, material-handling, and packaging. _____ is a channel of the supply chain which adds the value of time and place utility.
 a. Power III
 b. 6-3-5 Brainwriting
 c. 180SearchAssistant
 d. Logistics

18. _____ is a broad label that refers to any individuals or households that use goods and services generated within the economy The concept of a _____ is used in different contexts, so that the usage and significance of the term may vary.

A _____ is a person who uses any product or service.

 a. 180SearchAssistant
 b. Power III
 c. 6-3-5 Brainwriting
 d. Consumer

19. The _____ is a professional association for marketers. As of 2008 it had approximately 40,000 members. There are collegiate chapters on 250 campuses.
 a. AMAX
 b. ACNielsen
 c. ADTECH
 d. American Marketing Association

20. A supply chain is the system of organizations, people, technology, activities, information and resources involved in moving a product or service from _____ to customer. Supply chain activities transform natural resources, raw materials and components into a finished product that is delivered to the end customer. In sophisticated supply chain systems, used products may re-enter the supply chain at any point where residual value is recyclable.

a. Product line extension
b. Bringin' Home the Oil
c. Rebate
d. Supplier

21. _____ is a recursive process where two or more people or organizations work together toward an intersection of common goals -- for example, an intellectual endeavor that is creative in nature--by sharing knowledge, learning and building consensus. _____ does not require leadership and can sometimes bring better results through decentralization and egalitarianism. In particular, teams that work collaboratively can obtain greater resources, recognition and reward when facing competition for finite resources._____ is also present in opposing goals exhibiting the notion of adversarial _____, though this notion is atypical of the annotation that people have given towards their understanding of _____.
 a. Power III
 b. Collaboration
 c. 6-3-5 Brainwriting
 d. 180SearchAssistant

22. _____, also referred to as i-marketing, web marketing, online marketing is the marketing of products or services over the Internet.

The Internet has brought many unique benefits to marketing, one of which being lower costs for the distribution of information and media to a global audience. The interactive nature of _____, both in terms of providing instant response and eliciting responses, is a unique quality of the medium.

 a. Internet marketing
 b. ACNielsen
 c. AMAX
 d. ADTECH

23. A _____ is a type of business entity in which partners (owners) share with each other the profits or losses of the business undertaking in which all have invested. _____s are often favored over corporations for taxation purposes, as the _____ structure does not generally incur a tax on profits before it is distributed to the partners (i.e. there is no dividend tax levied.) However, depending on the _____ structure and the jurisdiction in which it operates, owners of a _____ may be exposed to greater personal liability than they would as shareholders of a corporation.
 a. Fair Debt Collection Practices Act
 b. Competition law
 c. Brand piracy
 d. Partnership

24. _____ is a rivalry between individuals, groups, nations for territory, a niche, or allocation of resources. It arises whenever two or more parties strive for a goal which cannot be shared. _____ occurs naturally between living organisms which co-exist in the same environment.

   a. Competition
   b. Price fixing
   c. Non-price competition
   d. Price competition

25. A _____ is a collection of symbols, experiences and associations connected with a product, a service, a person or any other artifact or entity.

_____s have become increasingly important components of culture and the economy, now being described as 'cultural accessories and personal philosophies'.

Some people distinguish the psychological aspect of a _____ from the experiential aspect.

   a. Brand
   b. Store brand
   c. Brand equity
   d. Brandable software

26. _____ is an advertisement in which a particular product specifically mentions a competitor by name for the express purpose of showing why the competitor is inferior to the product naming it.

This should not be confused with parody advertisements, where a fictional product is being advertised for the purpose of poking fun at the particular advertisement, nor should it be confused with the use of a coined brand name for the purpose of comparing the product without actually naming an actual competitor. ('Wikipedia tastes better and is less filling than the Encyclopedia Galactica.')

In the 1980s, during what has been referred to as the cola wars, soft-drink manufacturer Pepsi ran a series of advertisements where people, caught on hidden camera, in a blind taste test, chose Pepsi over rival Coca-Cola.

   a. GL-70
   b. Comparative advertising
   c. Heavy-up
   d. Cost per conversion

Chapter 4. Research Design, Exploratory Research, and Qualitative Data   21

1. _____ describes data and characteristics about the population or phenomenon being studied. _____ answers the questions who, what, where, when and how.

Although the data description is factual, accurate and systematic, the research cannot describe what caused a situation.

   a. Sampling error
   b. Power III
   c. Two-tailed test
   d. Descriptive research

2. _____ is a type of research conducted because a problem has not been clearly defined. _____ helps determine the best research design, data collection method and selection of subjects. Given its fundamental nature, _____ often concludes that a perceived problem does not actually exist.
   a. Exploratory research
   b. IDDEA
   c. ACNielsen
   d. Intent scale translation

3. A number of different _____s are indicated below.

   - Randomized controlled trial
     - Double-blind randomized trial
     - Single-blind randomized trial
     - Non-blind trial
   - Nonrandomized trial (quasi-experiment)
     - Interrupted time series design (measures on a sample or a series of samples from the same population are obtained several times before and after a manipulated event or a naturally occurring event) - considered a type of quasi-experiment

   - Cohort study
     - Prospective cohort
     - Retrospective cohort
     - Time series study
   - Case-control study
     - Nested case-control study
   - Cross-sectional study
     - Community survey (a type of cross-sectional study)

When choosing a _____, many factors must be taken into account. Different types of studies are subject to different types of bias. For example, recall bias is likely to occur in cross-sectional or case-control studies where subjects are asked to recall exposure to risk factors.

Chapter 4. Research Design, Exploratory Research, and Qualitative Data

   a. Longitudinal studies
   b. 180SearchAssistant
   c. Study design
   d. Power III

4. _____ is a field of inquiry that crosscuts disciplines and subject matters . _____ers aim to gather an in-depth understanding of human behavior and the reasons that govern such behavior. The discipline investigates the why and how of decision making, not just what, where, when.
   a. Power III
   b. 180SearchAssistant
   c. 6-3-5 Brainwriting
   d. Qualitative research

5. _____ refer to a collection of facts usually collected as the result of experience, observation or experiment or a set of premises. This may consist of numbers, words particularly as measurements or observations of a set of variables. _____ are often viewed as a lowest level of abstraction from which information and knowledge are derived.
   a. Data
   b. Sample size
   c. Pearson product-moment correlation coefficient
   d. Mean

6. A _____ is a form of qualitative research in which a group of people are asked about their attitude towards a product, service, concept, advertisement, idea, or packaging. Questions are asked in an interactive group setting where participants are free to talk with other group members.

Ernest Dichter originated the idea of having a 'group therapy' for products and this process is what became known as a _____.

   a. Logit analysis
   b. Marketing research process
   c. Cross tabulation
   d. Focus group

7. _____ is a mathematical science pertaining to the collection, analysis, interpretation or explanation, and presentation of data. It also provides tools for prediction and forecasting based on data. It is applicable to a wide variety of academic disciplines, from the natural and social sciences to the humanities, government and business.

Chapter 4. Research Design, Exploratory Research, and Qualitative Data

   a. Statistics
   b. Null hypothesis
   c. Type I error
   d. Median

8. _____ is the process of comparing the cost, cycle time, productivity, or quality of a specific process or method to another that is widely considered to be an industry standard or best practice. The result is often a business case for making changes in order to make improvements. The term _____ was first used by cobblers to measure ones feet for shoes.
   a. Switching cost
   b. Strategic group
   c. Benchmarking
   d. Business strategy

9. An _____ is one type of focus group, and is a sub-set of online research methods.

A moderator invites prescreened, qualified respondents who represent the target of interest to log on to conferencing software at a pre-arranged time and to take part in an _____. Some researchers will offer incentives for participating but this raises a number of ethical questions.

   a. Online Focus group
   b. Automated surveys
   c. Intangibility
   d. Engagement

10. _____ is the identity of a group or culture, or of an individual as far as one is influenced by one's belonging to a group or culture. _____ is similar to and has overlaps with, but is not synonymous with, identity politics.

There are modern questions of culture that are transferred into questions of identity.

   a. 6-3-5 Brainwriting
   b. 180SearchAssistant
   c. Power III
   d. Cultural identity

11. _____ are used for a variety of social and professional groups interacting via the Internet. It does not necessarily mean that there is a strong bond among the members, although Howard Rheingold, author of the book of the same name, mentions that _____ form 'when people carry on public discussions long enough, with sufficient human feeling, to form webs of personal relationships'. An email distribution list may have hundreds of members and the communication which takes place may be merely informational (questions and answers are posted), but members may remain relative strangers and the membership turnover rate could be high.

   a. Virtual communities
   b. 6-3-5 Brainwriting
   c. Power III
   d. 180SearchAssistant

12. _____ is an investment technique that requires investors to purchase multiple financial products with different maturity dates.

_____ avoids the risk of reinvesting a big portion of assets in an unfavorable financial environment. For example, a person has both a 2015 matured CD and a 2018 matured CD.

   a. 6-3-5 Brainwriting
   b. Laddering
   c. 180SearchAssistant
   d. Power III

13. _____ is a common word game involving an exchange of words that are associated together.

Once an original word has been chosen, usually randomly or arbitrarily, a player will find a word that they associate with it and make it known to all the players, usually by saying it aloud or writing it down as the next item on a list of words so far used. The next player must then do the same with this previous word.

   a. Word association
   b. 6-3-5 Brainwriting
   c. Power III
   d. 180SearchAssistant

14. _____ is the conveying of events in words, images, and sounds often by improvisation or embellishment. Stories or narratives have been shared in every culture and in every land as a means of entertainment, education, preservation of culture and in order to instill moral values. Crucial elements of stories and _____ include plot and characters, as well as the narrative point of view.

a. 6-3-5 Brainwriting
b. Power III
c. Storytelling
d. 180SearchAssistant

15. The general definition of an _____ is an evaluation of a person, organization, system, process, project or product. _____s are performed to ascertain the validity and reliability of information; also to provide an assessment of a system's internal control. The goal of an _____ is to express an opinion on the person/organization/system (etc) in question, under evaluation based on work done on a test basis.
   a. AMAX
   b. Audit
   c. ACNielsen
   d. ADTECH

16. _____ is either an activity of a living being (such as a human), consisting of receiving knowledge of the outside world through the senses, or the recording of data using scientific instruments. The term may also refer to any datum collected during this activity.

The scientific method requires _____s of nature to formulate and test hypotheses.

   a. ACNielsen
   b. AMAX
   c. Observation
   d. ADTECH

17. Mystery shopping or Mystery Consumer is a tool used by market research companies to measure quality of retail service or gather specific information about products and services. _____ posing as normal customers perform specific tasks-- such as purchasing a product, asking questions, registering complaints or behaving in a certain way - and then provide detailed reports or feedback about their experiences.

Mystery shopping began in the 1940s as a way to measure employee integrity.

   a. Mystery shopping
   b. Market research
   c. Mystery shoppers
   d. Questionnaire

18. _____ is a genre of writing that uses fieldwork to provide a descriptive study of human societies. _____ presents the results of a holistic research method founded on the idea that a system's properties cannot necessarily be accurately understood independently of each other. The genre has both formal and historical connections to travel writing and colonial office reports.
   a. ADTECH
   b. ACNielsen
   c. AMAX
   d. Ethnography

19. _____ is a standard point of view or personal prejudice. especially when the tendency interferes with the ability to be impartial, unprejudiced, or objective. The term _____ed is used to describe an action, judgment, or other outcome influenced by a prejudged perspective.
   a. Power III
   b. 180SearchAssistant
   c. 6-3-5 Brainwriting
   d. Bias

Chapter 5. Descriptive Research

1. _____ describes data and characteristics about the population or phenomenon being studied. _____ answers the questions who, what, where, when and how.

Although the data description is factual, accurate and systematic, the research cannot describe what caused a situation.

   a. Sampling error
   b. Two-tailed test
   c. Power III
   d. Descriptive research

2. _____ form a class of research methods that involve observation of some subset of a population of items all at the same time, in which, groups can be compared at different ages with respect of independent variables, such as IQ and memory. The fundamental difference between cross-sectional and longitudinal studies is that _____ take place at a single point in time and that a longitudinal study involves a series of measurements taken over a period of time. Both are a type of observational study.
   a. 180SearchAssistant
   b. Longitudinal studies
   c. Power III
   d. Cross-sectional studies

3. A _____ is a collection of symbols, experiences and associations connected with a product, a service, a person or any other artifact or entity.

_____s have become increasingly important components of culture and the economy, now being described as 'cultural accessories and personal philosophies'.

Some people distinguish the psychological aspect of a _____ from the experiential aspect.

   a. Brand equity
   b. Brand
   c. Brandable software
   d. Store brand

4. _____, in marketing, consists of a consumer's commitment to repurchase the brand and can be demonstrated by repeated buying of a product or service or other positive behaviors such as word of mouth advocacy. True _____ implies that the consumer is willing, at least on occasion, to put aside their own desires in the interest of the brand. _____ has been proclaimed by some to be the ultimate goal of marketing.

a. Trade Symbols
b. Brand implementation
c. Brand awareness
d. Brand loyalty

5. _____ is defined by the American _____ Association as the activity, set of institutions, and processes for creating, communicating, delivering, and exchanging offerings that have value for customers, clients, partners, and society at large. The term developed from the original meaning which referred literally to going to market, as in shopping, or going to a market to sell goods or services.

_____ practice tends to be seen as a creative industry, which includes advertising, distribution and selling.

a. Marketing
b. Marketing myopia
c. Product naming
d. Customer acquisition management

6. Consumer market research is a form of applied sociology that concentrates on understanding the behaviours, whims and preferences, of consumers in a market-based economy, and aims to understand the effects and comparative success of marketing campaigns. The field of consumer _____ as a statistical science was pioneered by Arthur Nielsen with the founding of the ACNielsen Company in 1923 .

Thus _____ is the systematic and objective identification, collection, analysis, and dissemination of information for the purpose of assisting management in decision making related to the identification and solution of problems and opportunities in marketing.

a. Logit analysis
b. Marketing research process
c. Marketing research
d. Focus group

Chapter 6. Causal Designs

1. _____ denotes a necessary relationship between one event and another event (called effect) which is the direct consequence of the first.

While this informal understanding suffices in everyday use, the philosophical analysis of how best to characterize _____ extends over millennia. In the western philosophical tradition explicit discussion stretches back at least as far as Aristotle, and the topic remains a staple in contemporary philosophy journals.

   a. Causality
   b. 6-3-5 Brainwriting
   c. Power III
   d. 180SearchAssistant

2. In calculus, a function f defined on a subset of the real numbers with real values is called _____, if for all x and y such that $x \leq y$ one has $f(x) \leq f(y)$, so f preserves the order. In layman's terms, the sign of the slope is always positive (the curve tending upwards) or zero (i.e., non-decreasing, or asymptotic, or depicted as a horizontal, flat line) Likewise, a function is called monotonically decreasing (non-increasing) if, whenever $x \leq y$, then $f(x) \geq f(y)$, so it reverses the order.
   a. 180SearchAssistant
   b. Monotonic
   c. 6-3-5 Brainwriting
   d. Power III

3. A _____ is any statistical hypothesis test in which the test statistic has a chi-square distribution when the null hypothesis is true, or any in which the probability distribution of the test statistic (assuming the null hypothesis is true) can be made to approximate a chi-square distribution as closely as desired by making the sample size large enough.

Some examples of chi-squared tests where the chi-square distribution is only approximately valid:

  - Pearson's _____, also known as the chi-square goodness-of-fit test or _____ for independence. When mentioned without any modifiers or without other precluding context, this test is usually understood.
  - Yates' _____, also known as Yates' correction for continuity.
  - Mantel-Haenszel _____.
  - Linear-by-linear association _____.
  - The portmanteau test in time-series analysis, testing for the presence of autocorrelation
  - Likelihood-ratio tests in general statistical modelling, for testing whether there is evidence of the need to move from a simple model to a more complicated one (where the simple model is nested within the complicated one.)

One case where the distribution of the test statistic is an exact chi-square distribution is the test that the variance of a normally-distributed population has a given value based on a sample variance. Such a test is uncommon in practice because values of variances to test against are seldom known exactly.

If a sample of size n is taken from a population having a normal distribution, then there is a well-known result which allows a test to be made of whether the variance of the population has a pre-determined value.

   a. Randomization
   b. Type I error
   c. Confounding variables
   d. Chi-square test

4. _____s are used in open sentences. For instance, in the formula x + 1 = 5, x is a _____ which represents an 'unknown' number. _____s are often represented by letters of the Roman alphabet, or those of other alphabets, such as Greek, and use other special symbols.
   a. Quantitative
   b. Variable
   c. Personalization
   d. Book of business

5. _____ describes data and characteristics about the population or phenomenon being studied. _____ answers the questions who, what, where, when and how.

Although the data description is factual, accurate and systematic, the research cannot describe what caused a situation.

   a. Power III
   b. Descriptive research
   c. Sampling error
   d. Two-tailed test

6. _____ is a type of research conducted because a problem has not been clearly defined. _____ helps determine the best research design, data collection method and selection of subjects. Given its fundamental nature, _____ often concludes that a perceived problem does not actually exist.
   a. IDDEA
   b. Exploratory research
   c. ACNielsen
   d. Intent scale translation

Chapter 6. Causal Designs

7. A _____ applies the scientific method to experimentally examine an intervention in the real world (or as many experimental economists like to say, naturally-occurring environments) rather than in the laboratory. _____s, like lab experiments, generally randomize subjects (or other sampling units) into treatment and control groups and compare outcomes between these groups. Clinical trials of pharmaceuticals are one example of _____s.

   a. 180SearchAssistant
   b. Response variable
   c. Power III
   d. Field experiment

8. _____ are variables other than the independent variable that may bear any effect on the behavior of the subject being studied.

   _____ are often classified into three main types:

   1. Subject variables, which are the characteristics of the individuals being studied that might affect their actions. These variables include age, gender, health status, mood, background, etc.
   2. Experimental variables are characteristics of the persons conducting the experiment which might influence how a person behaves. Gender, the presence of racial discrimination, language, or other factors may qualify as such variables.
   3. Situational variables are features of the environment in which the study or research was conducted, which have a bearing on the outcome of the experiment in a negative way. Included are the air temperature, level of activity, lighting, and the time of day.

   There are two strategies of controlling _____. Either a potentially influential variable is kept the same for all subjects in the research, or they balance the variables in a group.

   Take for example an experiment, in which a salesperson sells clothing on a door-to-door basis.

   a. ACNielsen
   b. AMAX
   c. ADTECH
   d. Extraneous variables

9. In economics, an externality or spillover of an economic transaction is an impact on a party that is not directly involved in the transaction. In such a case, prices do not reflect the full costs or benefits in production or consumption of a product or service. A positive impact is called an _____ benefit, while a negative impact is called an _____ cost.

a. ADTECH
b. AMAX
c. ACNielsen
d. External

10. _____ is the validity of generalized (causal) inferences in scientific studies, usually based on experiments as experimental validity.

Inferences about cause-effect relationships based on a specific scientific study are said to possess _____ if they may be generalized from the unique and idiosyncratic settings, procedures and participants to other populations and conditions Causal inferences said to possess high degrees of _____ can reasonably be expected to apply (a) to the target population of the study (i.e. from which the sample was drawn) (also referred to as population validity), and (b) to the universe of other populations (e.g. across time and space.)

The most common loss of _____ comes from the fact that experiments using human participants often employ small samples obtained from a single geographic location or with idiosyncratic features (e.g. volunteers.)

a. ACNielsen
b. ADTECH
c. AMAX
d. External validity

11. _____ is the validity of (causal) inferences in scientific studies, usually based on experiments as experimental validity .

Inferences are said to possess _____ if a causal relation between two variables is properly demonstrated . A causal inference may be based on a relation when three criteria are satisfied:

1. the 'cause' precedes the 'effect' in time (temporal precedence),
2. the 'cause' and the 'effect' are related (covariation), and
3. there are no plausible alternative explanations for the observed covariation (nonspuriousness) .

In scientific experimental settings, researchers often manipulate a variable (the independent variable) to see what effect it has on a second variable (the dependent variable) For example, a researcher might, for different experimental groups, manipulate the dosage of a particular drug between groups to see what effect it has on health. In this example, the researcher wants to make a causal inference, namely, that different doses of the drug may be held responsible for observed changes or differences.

a. ADTECH
b. ACNielsen
c. Internal validity
d. AMAX

12. _____ is a standard point of view or personal prejudice. especially when the tendency interferes with the ability to be impartial, unprejudiced, or objective. The term _____ed is used to describe an action, judgment, or other outcome influenced by a prejudged perspective.

a. Power III
b. 180SearchAssistant
c. Bias
d. 6-3-5 Brainwriting

13. In the mathematical discipline of graph theory a _____ or edge-independent set in a graph is a set of edges without common vertices. It may also be an entire graph consisting of edges without common vertices.

Given a graph G = (V,E), a _____ M in G is a set of pairwise non-adjacent edges; that is, no two edges share a common vertex.

a. 6-3-5 Brainwriting
b. Power III
c. 180SearchAssistant
d. Matching

14. _____ is the process of making something random; this means:

- Generating a random permutation of a sequence (such as when shuffling cards.)
- Selecting a random sample of a population (important in statistical sampling.)
- Generating random numbers: see Random number generation.
- Transforming a data stream using a scrambler in telecommunications.

_____ is used extensively in the field of gambling (or generally being random.) Imperfect _____ may allow a skilled gambler to have an advantage, so much research has been devoted to effective _____. A classic example of _____ is shuffling playing cards.

_____ is a core principle in the statistical theory of design of experiments.

a. Standard deviation
b. Statistics
c. Sample size
d. Randomization

15. _____ is a distortion of evidence or data that arises from the way that the data are collected. It is sometimes referred to as the selection effect. The term _____ most often refers to the distortion of a statistical analysis, due to the method of collecting samples.
  a. Power III
  b. 180SearchAssistant
  c. Selection bias
  d. Systematic sampling

16. _____ is a field of inquiry that crosscuts disciplines and subject matters . _____ers aim to gather an in-depth understanding of human behavior and the reasons that govern such behavior. The discipline investigates the why and how of decision making, not just what, where, when.
  a. 6-3-5 Brainwriting
  b. 180SearchAssistant
  c. Power III
  d. Qualitative research

17. The _____ is a professional association for marketers. As of 2008 it had approximately 40,000 members. There are collegiate chapters on 250 campuses.
  a. ADTECH
  b. ACNielsen
  c. American Marketing Association
  d. AMAX

18. _____ is defined by the American _____ Association as the activity, set of institutions, and processes for creating, communicating, delivering, and exchanging offerings that have value for customers, clients, partners, and society at large. The term developed from the original meaning which referred literally to going to market, as in shopping, or going to a market to sell goods or services.

_____ practice tends to be seen as a creative industry, which includes advertising, distribution and selling.

a. Customer acquisition management
b. Marketing myopia
c. Product naming
d. Marketing

19. Consumer market research is a form of applied sociology that concentrates on understanding the behaviours, whims and preferences, of consumers in a market-based economy, and aims to understand the effects and comparative success of marketing campaigns. The field of consumer _____ as a statistical science was pioneered by Arthur Nielsen with the founding of the ACNielsen Company in 1923 .

Thus _____ is the systematic and objective identification, collection, analysis, and dissemination of information for the purpose of assisting management in decision making related to the identification and solution of problems and opportunities in marketing.

a. Marketing research process
b. Focus group
c. Logit analysis
d. Marketing research

20. A _____, in the field of business and marketing, is a geographic region or demographic group used to gauge the viability of a product or service in the mass market prior to a wide scale roll-out. The criteria used to judge the acceptability of a _____ region or group include:

1. a population that is demographically similar to the proposed target market; and
2. relative isolation from densely populated media markets so that advertising to the test audience can be efficient and economical.

The _____ ideally aims to duplicate 'everything' - promotion and distribution as well as `product' - on a smaller scale. The technique replicates, typically in one area, what is planned to occur in a national launch; and the results are very carefully monitored, so that they can be extrapolated to projected national results. The `area' may be any one of the following:

- Television area
- Test town
- Residential neighborhood
- Test site

Chapter 6. Causal Designs

A number of decisions have to be taken about any _____:

- Which _____?
- What is to be tested?
- How long a test?
- What are the success criteria?

The simple go or no-go decision, together with the related reduction of risk, is normally the main justification for the expense of _____s. At the same time, however, such _____s can be used to test specific elements of a new product's marketing mix; possibly the version of the product itself, the promotional message and media spend, the distribution channels and the price.

   a. Preadolescence
   b. 180SearchAssistant
   c. Power III
   d. Test market

21. In economics, business, retail, and accounting, a _____ is the value of money that has been used up to produce something, and hence is not available for use anymore. In economics, a _____ is an alternative that is given up as a result of a decision. In business, the _____ may be one of acquisition, in which case the amount of money expended to acquire it is counted as _____.
   a. Cost
   b. Transaction cost
   c. Variable cost
   d. Fixed costs

22. _____ refer to a collection of facts usually collected as the result of experience, observation or experiment or a set of premises. This may consist of numbers, words particularly as measurements or observations of a set of variables. _____ are often viewed as a lowest level of abstraction from which information and knowledge are derived.
   a. Data
   b. Mean
   c. Sample size
   d. Pearson product-moment correlation coefficient

23. Combining Existing _____ Sources with New Primary Data Sources

Imagine that we could get hold of a good collection of surveys taken in earlier years, such as detailed studies about changes going on in this phase and hopefully additional studies in the years to come. Analyzing this data base over time could give us a good picture of what changes actually have taken place in the orientation of the population and of the extent to which new technical concepts did have an impact on subgroups of the population. Furthermore, data archives can help to prepare studies on change over time by monitoring what questions have been asked in earlier years and alerting principal investigators to important questions which should be repeated in planned research projects.

   a. Secondary data
   b. 180SearchAssistant
   c. Power III
   d. 6-3-5 Brainwriting

24. _____ is the imitation of some real thing, state of affairs, or process. The act of simulating something generally entails representing certain key characteristics or behaviors of a selected physical or abstract system.

_____ is used in many contexts, including the modeling of natural systems or human systems in order to gain insight into their functioning.

   a. Power III
   b. 180SearchAssistant
   c. 6-3-5 Brainwriting
   d. Simulation

25. _____ is a form of communication that typically attempts to persuade potential customers to purchase or to consume more of a particular brand of product or service. 'While now central to the contemporary global economy and the reproduction of global production networks, it is only quite recently that _____ has been more than a marginal influence on patterns of sales and production. The formation of modern _____ was intimately bound up with the emergence of new forms of monopoly capitalism around the end of the 19th and beginning of the 20th century as one element in corporate strategies to create, organize and where possible control markets, especially for mass produced consumer goods.
   a. ACNielsen
   b. AMAX
   c. ADTECH
   d. Advertising

Chapter 6. Causal Designs

26. _____ consists of the processes a company uses to track and organize its contacts with its current and prospective customers. _____ software is used to support these processes; information about customers and customer interactions can be entered, stored and accessed by employees in different company departments. Typical _____ goals are to improve services provided to customers, and to use customer contact information for targeted marketing.
   a. Customer Relationship Management
   b. Commercialization
   c. Product bundling
   d. Demand generation

27. Customer _____ consists of the processes a company uses to track and organize its contacts with its current and prospective customers. CRelationship management software is used to support these processes; information about customers and customer interactions can be entered, stored and accessed by employees in different company departments. Typical CRelationship management goals are to improve services provided to customers, and to use customer contact information for targeted marketing.
   a. Product bundling
   b. Green marketing
   c. Relationship Management
   d. Marketing

28. _____ is a genre of writing that uses fieldwork to provide a descriptive study of human societies. _____ presents the results of a holistic research method founded on the idea that a system's properties cannot necessarily be accurately understood independently of each other. The genre has both formal and historical connections to travel writing and colonial office reports.
   a. Ethnography
   b. ACNielsen
   c. AMAX
   d. ADTECH

Chapter 7. Data Collection: Secondary Data

1. _____ is a term for unprocessed data, it is also known as primary data. It is a relative term _____ can be input to a computer program or used in manual analysis procedures such as gathering statistics from a survey.
   a. Shoppers Food ' Pharmacy
   b. Raw data
   c. Product manager
   d. Chief marketing officer

2. Combining Existing _____ Sources with New Primary Data Sources

Imagine that we could get hold of a good collection of surveys taken in earlier years, such as detailed studies about changes going on in this phase and hopefully additional studies in the years to come. Analyzing this data base over time could give us a good picture of what changes actually have taken place in the orientation of the population and of the extent to which new technical concepts did have an impact on subgroups of the population. Furthermore, data archives can help to prepare studies on change over time by monitoring what questions have been asked in earlier years and alerting principal investigators to important questions which should be repeated in planned research projects.

   a. 180SearchAssistant
   b. 6-3-5 Brainwriting
   c. Power III
   d. Secondary data

3. _____ refer to a collection of facts usually collected as the result of experience, observation or experiment or a set of premises. This may consist of numbers, words particularly as measurements or observations of a set of variables. _____ are often viewed as a lowest level of abstraction from which information and knowledge are derived.
   a. Pearson product-moment correlation coefficient
   b. Mean
   c. Sample size
   d. Data

4. In economics, business, retail, and accounting, a _____ is the value of money that has been used up to produce something, and hence is not available for use anymore. In economics, a _____ is an alternative that is given up as a result of a decision. In business, the _____ may be one of acquisition, in which case the amount of money expended to acquire it is counted as _____.
   a. Variable cost
   b. Fixed costs
   c. Transaction cost
   d. Cost

Chapter 7. Data Collection: Secondary Data

5. The _____ is a publication of the United States Census Bureau, an agency of the United States Department of Commerce. Published annually since 1878, the statistics describe social and economic conditions in the United States.

In 1975 a two volume Historical Statistics of the United States, Colonial Times to 1970 Bicentennial Edition was published.

   a. 180SearchAssistant
   b. Power III
   c. 6-3-5 Brainwriting
   d. Statistical Abstract of the United States

6. _____ is defined by the American _____ Association as the activity, set of institutions, and processes for creating, communicating, delivering, and exchanging offerings that have value for customers, clients, partners, and society at large. The term developed from the original meaning which referred literally to going to market, as in shopping, or going to a market to sell goods or services.

_____ practice tends to be seen as a creative industry, which includes advertising, distribution and selling.

   a. Marketing
   b. Marketing myopia
   c. Product naming
   d. Customer acquisition management

7. _____ is an advertisement in which a particular product specifically mentions a competitor by name for the express purpose of showing why the competitor is inferior to the product naming it.

This should not be confused with parody advertisements, where a fictional product is being advertised for the purpose of poking fun at the particular advertisement, nor should it be confused with the use of a coined brand name for the purpose of comparing the product without actually naming an actual competitor. ('Wikipedia tastes better and is less filling than the Encyclopedia Galactica.')

In the 1980s, during what has been referred to as the cola wars, soft-drink manufacturer Pepsi ran a series of advertisements where people, caught on hidden camera, in a blind taste test, chose Pepsi over rival Coca-Cola.

   a. GL-70
   b. Cost per conversion
   c. Heavy-up
   d. Comparative advertising

Chapter 7. Data Collection: Secondary Data   41

8. In economics, an externality or spillover of an economic transaction is an impact on a party that is not directly involved in the transaction. In such a case, prices do not reflect the full costs or benefits in production or consumption of a product or service. A positive impact is called an _____ benefit, while a negative impact is called an _____ cost.
   a. External
   b. ACNielsen
   c. AMAX
   d. ADTECH

9. _____s are structured marketing efforts that reward, and therefore encourage, loyal buying behaviour -- behaviour which is potentially of benefit to the firm.

In marketing generally and in retailing more specifically, a loyalty card, rewards card, points card, advantage card, or club card is a plastic or paper card, visually similar to a credit card or debit card, that identifies the card holder as a member in a _____. Loyalty cards are a system of the loyalty business model.

   a. 6-3-5 Brainwriting
   b. 180SearchAssistant
   c. Power III
   d. Loyalty program

10. _____ is the examining of goods or services from retailers with the intent to purchase at that time. _____ is an activity of selection and/or purchase. In some contexts it is considered a leisure activity as well as an economic one.
   a. Discount store
   b. Khodebshchik
   c. Hawkers
   d. Shopping

11. _____ is the process of extracting hidden patterns from data. As more data is gathered, with the amount of data doubling every three years, _____ is becoming an increasingly important tool to transform this data into information. It is commonly used in a wide range of profiling practices, such as marketing, surveillance, fraud detection and scientific discovery.
   a. Structure mining
   b. Power III
   c. Data mining
   d. 180SearchAssistant

12. A _____ is a structured collection of records or data that is stored in a computer system. The structure is achieved by organizing the data according to a _____ model. The model in most common use today is the relational model.

a. Power III
b. 6-3-5 Brainwriting
c. 180SearchAssistant
d. Database

13. An _____ is the manufacturing of a good or service within a category. Although _____ is a broad term for any kind of economic production, in economics and urban planning _____ is a synonym for the secondary sector, which is a type of economic activity involved in the manufacturing of raw materials into goods and products.

There are four key industrial economic sectors: the primary sector, largely raw material extraction industries such as mining and farming; the secondary sector, involving refining, construction, and manufacturing; the tertiary sector, which deals with services (such as law and medicine) and distribution of manufactured goods; and the quaternary sector, a relatively new type of knowledge _____ focusing on technological research, design and development such as computer programming, and biochemistry.

a. Industry
b. ACNielsen
c. AMAX
d. ADTECH

14. _____s is the social science that studies the production, distribution, and consumption of goods and services. The term _____s comes from the Ancient Greek oá¼°κονομῖα from oá¼¶κος (oikos, 'house') + νÏŒμος (nomos, 'custom' or 'law'), hence 'rules of the house(hold)'. Current _____ models developed out of the broader field of political economy in the late 19th century, owing to a desire to use an empirical approach more akin to the physical sciences.

a. ACNielsen
b. Industrial organization
c. ADTECH
d. Economic

15. _____ is the state or fact of exclusive rights and control over property, which may be an object, land/real estate, or some other kind of property (like government-granted monopolies collectively referred to as intellectual property.) It is embodied in an _____ right also referred to as title.

_____ is the key building block in the development of the capitalist socio-economic system.

a. ACNielsen
b. AMAX
c. Ownership
d. ADTECH

16. _____, also referred to as i-marketing, web marketing, online marketing is the marketing of products or services over the Internet.

The Internet has brought many unique benefits to marketing, one of which being lower costs for the distribution of information and media to a global audience. The interactive nature of _____, both in terms of providing instant response and eliciting responses, is a unique quality of the medium.

a. ADTECH
b. ACNielsen
c. AMAX
d. Internet marketing

17. The _____ is a very large set of interlinked hypertext documents accessed via the Internet. With a Web browser, one can view Web pages that may contain text, images, videos, and other multimedia and navigate between them using hyperlinks. Using concepts from earlier hypertext systems, the _____ was begun in 1992 by the English physicist Sir Tim Berners-Lee, now the Director of the _____ Consortium, and Robert Cailliau, a Belgian computer scientist, while both were working at CERN in Geneva, Switzerland.
a. World Wide Web
b. 6-3-5 Brainwriting
c. Power III
d. 180SearchAssistant

18. _____ , according to Cornish, 'the process of acquiring and analyzing information in order to understand the market (both existing and potential customers); to determine the current and future needs and preferences, attitudes and behavior of the market; and to assess changes in the business environment that may affect the size and nature of the market in the future.' ('Product', 1997, p147.)

This figure shows how the interaction between variables from producers, communication channels, and consumers vary the effectiveness of _____ which affects the performance of the sales of a new product. The product is central in a circle because it helps to direct what information is gathered and how.

a. Market intelligence
b. Brand parity
c. Line extension
d. Co-branding

19. Consumer market research is a form of applied sociology that concentrates on understanding the behaviours, whims and preferences, of consumers in a market-based economy, and aims to understand the effects and comparative success of marketing campaigns. The field of consumer _____ as a statistical science was pioneered by Arthur Nielsen with the founding of the ACNielsen Company in 1923.

Thus _____ is the systematic and objective identification, collection, analysis, and dissemination of information for the purpose of assisting management in decision making related to the identification and solution of problems and opportunities in marketing.

a. Marketing research
b. Focus group
c. Marketing research process
d. Logit analysis

20. The _____ or _____ is used by business and government to classify and measure economic activity in Canada, Mexico and the United States. It has largely replaced the older Standard Industrial Classification system; however, certain government departments and agencies, such as the U.S. Securities and Exchange Commission (SEC), still use the SIC codes.

The _____ numbering system is a six-digit code.

a. Power III
b. North American Industry Classification System
c. 6-3-5 Brainwriting
d. 180SearchAssistant

21. _____ is a broad label that refers to any individuals or households that use goods and services generated within the economy. The concept of a _____ is used in different contexts, so that the usage and significance of the term may vary.

A _____ is a person who uses any product or service.

a. Power III
b. 180SearchAssistant
c. 6-3-5 Brainwriting
d. Consumer

22. The United States _____ is the government agency that is responsible for the United States Census. It also gathers other national demographic and economic data.
a. 6-3-5 Brainwriting
b. 180SearchAssistant
c. Census Bureau
d. Power III

23. _____ is the study of the Earth and its lands, features, inhabitants, and phenomena. A literal translation would be 'to describe or write about the Earth'. The first person to use the word '_____' was Eratosthenes .
a. 6-3-5 Brainwriting
b. Power III
c. 180SearchAssistant
d. Geography

24. A _____ captures, stores, analyzes, manages, and presents data that is linked to location.

In the strictest sense, the term describes any information system that integrates, stores, edits, analyzes, shares, and displays geographic information. In a more generic sense, _____ applications are tools that allow users to create interactive queries (user created searches), analyze spatial information, edit data, maps, and present the results of all these operations.

a. Geographic information system
b. Power III
c. 6-3-5 Brainwriting
d. 180SearchAssistant

25. _____, in strategic management and marketing, is the percentage or proportion of the total available market or market segment that is being serviced by a company. It can be expressed as a company's sales revenue (from that market) divided by the total sales revenue available in that market. It can also be expressed as a company's unit sales volume (in a market) divided by the total volume of units sold in that market.

a. Customer relationship management
b. Demand generation
c. Market share
d. Cyberdoc

26. The general definition of an _____ is an evaluation of a person, organization, system, process, project or product. _____s are performed to ascertain the validity and reliability of information; also to provide an assessment of a system's internal control. The goal of an _____ is to express an opinion on the person/organization/system (etc) in question, under evaluation based on work done on a test basis.
    a. ACNielsen
    b. AMAX
    c. ADTECH
    d. Audit

27. _____ is that part of statistical practice concerned with the selection of individual observations intended to yield some knowledge about a population of concern, especially for the purposes of statistical inference. Each observation measures one or more properties (weight, location, etc.) of an observable entity enumerated to distinguish objects or individuals.
    a. AStore
    b. Richard Buckminster 'Bucky' Fuller
    c. Sports Marketing Group
    d. Sampling

28. Human beings are also considered to be _____ because they have the ability to change raw materials into valuable _____. The term Human _____ can also be defined as the skills, energies, talents, abilities and knowledge that are used for the production of goods or the rendering of services. While taking into account human beings as _____, the following things have to be kept in mind:

    - The size of the population
    - The capabilities of the individuals in that population

    Many _____ cannot be consumed in their original form. They have to be processed in order to change them into more usable commodities.

    a. 6-3-5 Brainwriting
    b. 180SearchAssistant
    c. Resources
    d. Power III

29. _____ is a form of communication that typically attempts to persuade potential customers to purchase or to consume more of a particular brand of product or service. 'While now central to the contemporary global economy and the reproduction of global production networks, it is only quite recently that _____ has been more than a marginal influence on patterns of sales and production. The formation of modern _____ was intimately bound up with the emergence of new forms of monopoly capitalism around the end of the 19th and beginning of the 20th century as one element in corporate strategies to create, organize and where possible control markets, especially for mass produced consumer goods.
   a. ADTECH
   b. ACNielsen
   c. AMAX
   d. Advertising

30. A _____ is a form of qualitative research in which a group of people are asked about their attitude towards a product, service, concept, advertisement, idea, or packaging. Questions are asked in an interactive group setting where participants are free to talk with other group members.

Ernest Dichter originated the idea of having a 'group therapy' for products and this process is what became known as a _____.

   a. Marketing research process
   b. Cross tabulation
   c. Logit analysis
   d. Focus group

Chapter 8. Data Collection: Primary Data

1. _____ is a term for unprocessed data, it is also known as primary data. It is a relative term _____ can be input to a computer program or used in manual analysis procedures such as gathering statistics from a survey.
    a. Raw data
    b. Product manager
    c. Shoppers Food ' Pharmacy
    d. Chief marketing officer

2. _____ refer to a collection of facts usually collected as the result of experience, observation or experiment or a set of premises. This may consist of numbers, words particularly as measurements or observations of a set of variables. _____ are often viewed as a lowest level of abstraction from which information and knowledge are derived.
    a. Data
    b. Pearson product-moment correlation coefficient
    c. Mean
    d. Sample size

3. _____ was originally coined by Austrian psychologist Alfred Adler in 1929. The current broader sense of the word dates from 1961.

    In sociology, a _____ is the way a person lives.

    a. Power III
    b. 180SearchAssistant
    c. 6-3-5 Brainwriting
    d. Lifestyle

4. In the field of marketing, demographics, opinion research, and social research in general, _____ variables are any attributes relating to personality, values, attitudes, interests, or lifestyles. They are also called IAO variables . They can be contrasted with demographic variables (such as age and gender), behavioral variables (such as usage rate or loyalty), and bizographic variables (such as industry, seniority and functional area.)
    a. Psychographic
    b. Lifetime value
    c. Marketing myopia
    d. Business-to-business

5. The acronym _____, is a psychographic segmentation. It was developed in the 1970s to explain changing U.S. values and lifestyles. It has since been reworked to enhance its ability to predict consumer behavior.

Chapter 8. Data Collection: Primary Data

According to the _____ Framework, groups of people are arranged in a rectangle and are based on two dimensions. The vertical dimension segments people based on the degree to which they are innovative and have resources such as income, education, self-confidence, intelligence, leadership skills, and energy.

a. Power III
b. 180SearchAssistant
c. 6-3-5 Brainwriting
d. VALS

6. _____ is the set of reasons that determines one to engage in a particular behavior. The term is generally used for human _____ but, theoretically, it can be used to describe the causes for animal behavior as well
   a. 180SearchAssistant
   b. Role playing
   c. Motivation
   d. Power III

7. _____ is that part of statistical practice concerned with the selection of individual observations intended to yield some knowledge about a population of concern, especially for the purposes of statistical inference. Each observation measures one or more properties (weight, location, etc.) of an observable entity enumerated to distinguish objects or individuals.
   a. AStore
   b. Richard Buckminster 'Bucky' Fuller
   c. Sports Marketing Group
   d. Sampling

8. In environmental modeling and especially in hydrology, a _____ model means a model that is acceptably consistent with observed natural processes, i.e. that simulates well, for example, observed river discharge. It is a key concept of the so-called Generalized Likelihood Uncertainty Estimation (GLUE) methodology to quantify how uncertain environmental predictions are.
   a. Behavioral
   b. Power III
   c. 6-3-5 Brainwriting
   d. 180SearchAssistant

9. _____ is either an activity of a living being (such as a human), consisting of receiving knowledge of the outside world through the senses, or the recording of data using scientific instruments. The term may also refer to any datum collected during this activity.

Chapter 8. Data Collection: Primary Data

The scientific method requires _____s of nature to formulate and test hypotheses.

a. AMAX
b. ACNielsen
c. ADTECH
d. Observation

10. _____, also referred to as i-marketing, web marketing, online marketing is the marketing of products or services over the Internet.

The Internet has brought many unique benefits to marketing, one of which being lower costs for the distribution of information and media to a global audience. The interactive nature of _____, both in terms of providing instant response and eliciting responses, is a unique quality of the medium.

a. ADTECH
b. Internet marketing
c. AMAX
d. ACNielsen

11. The _____ is a very large set of interlinked hypertext documents accessed via the Internet. With a Web browser, one can view Web pages that may contain text, images, videos, and other multimedia and navigate between them using hyperlinks. Using concepts from earlier hypertext systems, the _____ was begun in 1992 by the English physicist Sir Tim Berners-Lee, now the Director of the _____ Consortium, and Robert Cailliau, a Belgian computer scientist, while both were working at CERN in Geneva, Switzerland.

a. World Wide Web
b. 6-3-5 Brainwriting
c. Power III
d. 180SearchAssistant

12. _____ is a term used to describe a process of preparing and collecting data - for example as part of a process improvement or similar project.

Chapter 8. Data Collection: Primary Data 51

_____ usually takes place early on in an improvement project, and is often formalised through a _____ Plan which often contains the following activity.

1. Pre collection activity - Agree goals, target data, definitions, methods
2. Collection - _____
3. Present Findings - usually involves some form of sorting analysis and/or presentation.

A formal _____ process is necessary as it ensures that data gathered is both defined and accurate and that subsequent decisions based on arguments embodied in the findings are valid . The process provides both a baseline from which to measure from and in certain cases a target on what to improve. Types of _____ 1-By mail questionnaires 2-By personal interview

- Six sigma
- Sampling (statistics)

a. Power III
b. 6-3-5 Brainwriting
c. 180SearchAssistant
d. Data collection

13. _____ is defined by the American _____ Association as the activity, set of institutions, and processes for creating, communicating, delivering, and exchanging offerings that have value for customers, clients, partners, and society at large. The term developed from the original meaning which referred literally to going to market, as in shopping, or going to a market to sell goods or services.

_____ practice tends to be seen as a creative industry, which includes advertising, distribution and selling.

a. Product naming
b. Marketing myopia
c. Customer acquisition management
d. Marketing

14. _____ , according to Cornish, 'the process of acquiring and analyzing information in order to understand the market (both existing and potential customers); to determine the current and future needs and preferences, attitudes and behavior of the market; and to assess changes in the business environment that may affect the size and nature of the market in the future.' ('Product', 1997, p147.)

This figure shows how the interaction between variables from producers, communication channels, and consumers vary the effectiveness of _____ which affects the performance of the sales of a new product. The product is central in a circle because it helps to direct what information is gathered and how.

a. Brand parity
b. Market intelligence
c. Line extension
d. Co-branding

15. In economics, business, retail, and accounting, a _____ is the value of money that has been used up to produce something, and hence is not available for use anymore. In economics, a _____ is an alternative that is given up as a result of a decision. In business, the _____ may be one of acquisition, in which case the amount of money expended to acquire it is counted as _____.
a. Variable cost
b. Transaction cost
c. Fixed costs
d. Cost

16. Combining Existing _____ Sources with New Primary Data Sources

Imagine that we could get hold of a good collection of surveys taken in earlier years, such as detailed studies about changes going on in this phase and hopefully additional studies in the years to come. Analyzing this data base over time could give us a good picture of what changes actually have taken place in the orientation of the population and of the extent to which new technical concepts did have an impact on subgroups of the population. Furthermore, data archives can help to prepare studies on change over time by monitoring what questions have been asked in earlier years and alerting principal investigators to important questions which should be repeated in planned research projects.

a. Power III
b. 180SearchAssistant
c. 6-3-5 Brainwriting
d. Secondary data

17. A _____ is a research instrument consisting of a series of questions and other prompts for the purpose of gathering information from respondents. Although they are often designed for statistical analysis of the responses, this is not always the case. The _____ was invented by Sir Francis Galton.

a. Market research
b. Mystery shoppers
c. Mystery shopping
d. Questionnaire

18. _____ is a broad label that refers to any individuals or households that use goods and services generated within the economy. The concept of a _____ is used in different contexts, so that the usage and significance of the term may vary.

A _____ is a person who uses any product or service.

a. 6-3-5 Brainwriting
b. Consumer
c. Power III
d. 180SearchAssistant

19. _____ is an advertisement in which a particular product specifically mentions a competitor by name for the express purpose of showing why the competitor is inferior to the product naming it.

This should not be confused with parody advertisements, where a fictional product is being advertised for the purpose of poking fun at the particular advertisement, nor should it be confused with the use of a coined brand name for the purpose of comparing the product without actually naming an actual competitor. ('Wikipedia tastes better and is less filling than the Encyclopedia Galactica.')

In the 1980s, during what has been referred to as the cola wars, soft-drink manufacturer Pepsi ran a series of advertisements where people, caught on hidden camera, in a blind taste test, chose Pepsi over rival Coca-Cola.

a. Heavy-up
b. Comparative advertising
c. Cost per conversion
d. GL-70

20. A _____ is a form of qualitative research in which a group of people are asked about their attitude towards a product, service, concept, advertisement, idea, or packaging. Questions are asked in an interactive group setting where participants are free to talk with other group members.

Ernest Dichter originated the idea of having a 'group therapy' for products and this process is what became known as a _____.

a. Cross tabulation
b. Logit analysis
c. Focus group
d. Marketing research process

21. _____ is a standard point of view or personal prejudice. especially when the tendency interferes with the ability to be impartial, unprejudiced, or objective. The term _____ed is used to describe an action, judgment, or other outcome influenced by a prejudged perspective.
   a. 180SearchAssistant
   b. 6-3-5 Brainwriting
   c. Power III
   d. Bias

22. _____ is the identity of a group or culture, or of an individual as far as one is influenced by one's belonging to a group or culture. _____ is similar to and has overlaps with, but is not synonymous with, identity politics.

There are modern questions of culture that are transferred into questions of identity.

   a. Cultural identity
   b. 180SearchAssistant
   c. Power III
   d. 6-3-5 Brainwriting

23. An _____ is a special-purpose computer system designed to perform one or a few dedicated functions, often with real-time computing constraints. It is usually embedded as part of a complete device including hardware and mechanical parts. In contrast, a general-purpose computer, such as a personal computer, can do many different tasks depending on programming.
   a. Embedded system
   b. ACNielsen
   c. AMAX
   d. ADTECH

24. _____ in survey research refers to the ratio of number of people who answered the survey divided by the number of people in the sample. It is usually expressed in the form of a percentage.

Example: if 1,000 surveys were sent by mail, and 257 were successfully completed and returned, then the _____ would be 25.7 %.

a. Reference value
b. Power III
c. Sentence completion tests
d. Response rate

Chapter 9. Questionnaires and Data-Collection Forms

1. A _____ is a research instrument consisting of a series of questions and other prompts for the purpose of gathering information from respondents. Although they are often designed for statistical analysis of the responses, this is not always the case. The _____ was invented by Sir Francis Galton.
   a. Questionnaire
   b. Mystery shopping
   c. Market research
   d. Mystery shoppers

2. A _____ is an explicit set of requirements to be satisfied by a material, product, or service.

In engineering, manufacturing, and business, it is vital for suppliers, purchasers, and users of materials, products, or services to understand and agree upon all requirements. A _____ is a type of a standard which is often referenced by a contract or procurement document.

   a. New product development
   b. Product optimization
   c. Product development
   d. Specification

3. The _____ is a professional association for marketers. As of 2008 it had approximately 40,000 members. There are collegiate chapters on 250 campuses.
   a. ACNielsen
   b. ADTECH
   c. AMAX
   d. American Marketing Association

4. In economics, business, retail, and accounting, a _____ is the value of money that has been used up to produce something, and hence is not available for use anymore. In economics, a _____ is an alternative that is given up as a result of a decision. In business, the _____ may be one of acquisition, in which case the amount of money expended to acquire it is counted as _____.
   a. Transaction cost
   b. Variable cost
   c. Fixed costs
   d. Cost

5. _____ is the identity of a group or culture, or of an individual as far as one is influenced by one's belonging to a group or culture. _____ is similar to and has overlaps with, but is not synonymous with, identity politics.

There are modern questions of culture that are transferred into questions of identity.

a. 6-3-5 Brainwriting
b. Power III
c. 180SearchAssistant
d. Cultural identity

6. _____ is defined by the American _____ Association as the activity, set of institutions, and processes for creating, communicating, delivering, and exchanging offerings that have value for customers, clients, partners, and society at large. The term developed from the original meaning which referred literally to going to market, as in shopping, or going to a market to sell goods or services.

_____ practice tends to be seen as a creative industry, which includes advertising, distribution and selling.

a. Customer acquisition management
b. Marketing myopia
c. Product naming
d. Marketing

7. Consumer market research is a form of applied sociology that concentrates on understanding the behaviours, whims and preferences, of consumers in a market-based economy, and aims to understand the effects and comparative success of marketing campaigns. The field of consumer _____ as a statistical science was pioneered by Arthur Nielsen with the founding of the ACNielsen Company in 1923 .

Thus _____ is the systematic and objective identification, collection, analysis, and dissemination of information for the purpose of assisting management in decision making related to the identification and solution of problems and opportunities in marketing.

a. Marketing research process
b. Logit analysis
c. Marketing research
d. Focus group

8. _____ refer to a collection of facts usually collected as the result of experience, observation or experiment or a set of premises. This may consist of numbers, words particularly as measurements or observations of a set of variables. _____ are often viewed as a lowest level of abstraction from which information and knowledge are derived.

a. Pearson product-moment correlation coefficient
b. Sample size
c. Mean
d. Data

9. A _____ is a form of qualitative research in which a group of people are asked about their attitude towards a product, service, concept, advertisement, idea, or packaging. Questions are asked in an interactive group setting where participants are free to talk with other group members.

Ernest Dichter originated the idea of having a 'group therapy' for products and this process is what became known as a _____.

   a. Cross tabulation
   b. Focus group
   c. Logit analysis
   d. Marketing research process

10. Combining Existing _____ Sources with New Primary Data Sources

Imagine that we could get hold of a good collection of surveys taken in earlier years, such as detailed studies about changes going on in this phase and hopefully additional studies in the years to come. Analyzing this data base over time could give us a good picture of what changes actually have taken place in the orientation of the population and of the extent to which new technical concepts did have an impact on subgroups of the population. Furthermore, data archives can help to prepare studies on change over time by monitoring what questions have been asked in earlier years and alerting principal investigators to important questions which should be repeated in planned research projects.

   a. Power III
   b. 180SearchAssistant
   c. 6-3-5 Brainwriting
   d. Secondary data

11. _____s are errors in measurement that lead to measured values being inconsistent when repeated measures of a constant attribute or quantity are taken. The word random indicates that they are inherently unpredictable, and have null expected value, namely, they are scattered about the true value, and tend to have null arithmetic mean when a measurement is repeated several times with the same instrument. All measurements are prone to _____.
   a. 180SearchAssistant
   b. Power III
   c. Systematic error
   d. Random error

12. _____ is that part of statistical practice concerned with the selection of individual observations intended to yield some knowledge about a population of concern, especially for the purposes of statistical inference. Each observation measures one or more properties (weight, location, etc.) of an observable entity enumerated to distinguish objects or individuals.

Chapter 9. Questionnaires and Data-Collection Forms

   a. AStore
   b. Sports Marketing Group
   c. Richard Buckminster 'Bucky' Fuller
   d. Sampling

13. _____ is a form of assessment in which respondents are asked to select one or more choices from a list. The _____ format is most frequently used in educational testing, in market research, and in elections-- when a person chooses between multiple candidates, parties, or policies. _____ testing is particularly popular in the United States.
   a. 6-3-5 Brainwriting
   b. 180SearchAssistant
   c. Power III
   d. Multiple choice

14. _____ is the difference between a measured value of quantity and its true value. In statistics, an error is not a 'mistake'. Variability is an inherent part of things being measured and of the measurement process.
   a. ADTECH
   b. Observational error
   c. ACNielsen
   d. AMAX

15. In common law systems that rely on testimony by witnesses, a _____ is a question that suggests the answer or contains the information the examiner is looking for. For example, this question is leading:

- You were at Duffy's bar on the night of July 15, weren't you?

It suggests that the witness was at Duffy's bar on the night in question. The same question in a non-leading form would be:

- Where were you on the night of July 15?

This form of question does not suggest to the witness the answer the examiner hopes to elicit.

_____s may often be answerable with a yes or no (though not all yes-no questions are leading), while non-_____s are open-ended. Depending on the circumstances _____s can be objectionable or proper.

Chapter 9. Questionnaires and Data-Collection Forms

a. Contract price
b. Substantive law
c. Leading question
d. Power III

16. _____ is a foundational element of logic and human reasoning. _____ posits the existence of a domain or set of elements, as well as one or more common characteristics shared by those elements. As such, it is the essential basis of all valid deductive inference.

a. 6-3-5 Brainwriting
b. Power III
c. Generalization
d. 180SearchAssistant

Chapter 10. Attitude Measurement

1. The '_____' is an expression which typically refers to the theory of scale types developed by the Harvard psychologist Stanley Smith Stevens In this article Stevens claimed that all measurement in science was conducted using four different types of numerical scales which he called 'nominal', 'ordinal', 'interval' and 'ratio'.
   a. 180SearchAssistant
   b. Levels of measurement
   c. 6-3-5 Brainwriting
   d. Power III

2. _____ is that part of statistical practice concerned with the selection of individual observations intended to yield some knowledge about a population of concern, especially for the purposes of statistical inference. Each observation measures one or more properties (weight, location, etc.) of an observable entity enumerated to distinguish objects or individuals.
   a. Sports Marketing Group
   b. Richard Buckminster 'Bucky' Fuller
   c. AStore
   d. Sampling

3. In algebra, the _____ of a polynomial with real or complex coefficients is a certain expression in the coefficients of the polynomial which is equal to zero if and only if the polynomial has a multiple root (i.e. a root with multiplicity greater than one) in the complex numbers. For example, the _____ of the quadratic polynomial

   $ax^2 + bx + c$ is $b^2 - 4ac$.

   The _____ of the cubic polynomial

   $ax^3 + bx^2 + cx + d$ is $b^2c^2 - 4ac^3 - 4b^3d - 27a^2d^2 + 18abcd$.

   a. Flighting
   b. Consumption Map
   c. Lifestyle center
   d. Discriminant

4. _____ describes the degree to which the operationalization is not similar to (diverges from) other operationalizations that it theoretically should not be similar to.

   Campbell and Fiske (1959) introduced the concept of _____ within their discussion on evaluating test validity. They stressed the importance of using both discriminant and convergent validation techniques when assessing new tests.

a. Convergent validity
b. Criterion validity
c. Predictive validity
d. Discriminant validity

5. _____ is either an activity of a living being (such as a human), consisting of receiving knowledge of the outside world through the senses, or the recording of data using scientific instruments. The term may also refer to any datum collected during this activity.

The scientific method requires _____s of nature to formulate and test hypotheses.

a. ACNielsen
b. ADTECH
c. AMAX
d. Observation

6. _____ is a way of expressing knowledge or belief that an event will occur or has occurred. In mathematics the concept has been given an exact meaning in _____ theory, that is used extensively in such areas of study as mathematics, statistics, finance, gambling, science, and philosophy to draw conclusions about the likelihood of potential events and the underlying mechanics of complex systems.

a. Heteroskedastic
b. Linear regression
c. Data
d. Probability

7. _____ is a type of a rating scale designed to measure the connotative meaning of objects, events, and concepts. The connotations are used to derive the attitude towards the given object, event or concept.

Osgood's _____ was designed to measure the connotative meaning of concepts.

a. Power III
b. Factor analysis
c. Likert scale
d. Semantic differential

8. In grammar, the _____ is the form of an adjective or adverb which denotes the degree or grade by which a person, thing and is used in this context with a subordinating conjunction, such as than, as...as, etc.

The structure of a _____ in English consists normally of the positive form of the adjective or adverb, plus the suffix -er e.g. 'he is taller than his father is', or 'the village is less picturesque than the town nearby'.

   a. 6-3-5 Brainwriting
   b. Power III
   c. 180SearchAssistant
   d. Comparative

9. _____s are errors in measurement that lead to measured values being inconsistent when repeated measures of a constant attribute or quantity are taken. The word random indicates that they are inherently unpredictable, and have null expected value, namely, they are scattered about the true value, and tend to have null arithmetic mean when a measurement is repeated several times with the same instrument. All measurements are prone to _____.
   a. 180SearchAssistant
   b. Random error
   c. Power III
   d. Systematic error

10. _____s are biases in measurement which lead to the situation where the mean of many separate measurements differs significantly from the actual value of the measured attribute. All measurements are prone to _____s, often of several different types. Sources of _____ may be imperfect calibration of measurement instruments, changes in the environment which interfere with the measurement process and sometimes imperfect methods of observation can be either zero error or percentage error.
   a. 180SearchAssistant
   b. Power III
   c. Systematic bias
   d. Systematic error

11. _____ is a parameter used in sociology, psychology, and other psychometric or behavioral sciences. _____ is demonstrated where a test correlates well with a measure that has previously been validated. The two measures may be for the same construct, or for different, but presumably related, constructs.
   a. Discriminant validity
   b. Criterion validity
   c. Construct validity
   d. Concurrent validity

Chapter 10. Attitude Measurement

12. In psychometrics, _____ refers to the extent to which a measure represents all facets of a given social construct. For example, a depression scale may lack _____ if it only assesses the affective dimension of depression but fails to take into account the behavioral dimension. An element of subjectivity exists in relation to determining _____, which requires a degree of agreement about what a particular personality trait such as extraversion represents.
   a. Criterion validity
   b. Content validity
   c. Predictive validity
   d. Convergent validity

13. _____ is a property of a test intended to measure something. The test is said to have _____ if it 'looks like' it is going to measure what it is supposed to measure. For instance, if you prepare a test to measure whether students can perform multiplication, and the people you show it to all agree that it looks like a good test of multiplication ability, you have shown the _____ of your test.
   a. Face validity
   b. Selective distortion
   c. Power III
   d. 180SearchAssistant

14. A _____ is a statement or claim that a particular event will occur in the future in more certain terms than a forecast. The etymology of this word is Latin . In regards to predicting the future Howard H. Stevenson Says, ' _____ is at least two things: Important and hard.' Important, because we have to act, and hard because we have to realize the future we want, and what is the best way to get there.
   a. Prediction
   b. Power III
   c. 180SearchAssistant
   d. 6-3-5 Brainwriting

15. In psychometrics, _____ is the extent to which a score on a scale or test predicts scores on some criterion measure.

For example, the validity of a cognitive test for job performance is the correlation between test scores and, for example, supervisor performance ratings. Such a cognitive test would have _____ if the observed correlation were statistically significant.

   a. Discriminant validity
   b. Predictive validity
   c. Criterion validity
   d. Convergent validity

Chapter 10. Attitude Measurement

16. In social science and psychometrics, _____ refers to whether a scale measures or correlates with a theorized psychological construct (such as 'fluid intelligence'.) It is related to the theoretical ideas behind the personality trait under consideration; a non-existent concept in the physical sense may be suggested as a method of organising how personality can be viewed. The unobservable idea of a unidimensional easier-to-harder dimension must be 'constructed' in the words of human language and graphics.
    a. Discriminant validity
    b. Predictive validity
    c. Criterion validity
    d. Construct validity

17. In the absence of a more specific context, convergence denotes the approach toward a definite value, as time goes on; or to a definite point, a common view or opinion, or toward a fixed or equilibrium state. _____ is the adjectival form, and also a noun meaning an iterative approximation.

In mathematics, convergence describes limiting behaviour, particularly of an infinite sequence or series, toward some limit.

    a. Good things come to those who wait
    b. Geo
    c. Strict liability
    d. Convergent

18. _____ is the degree to which an operation is similar to (converges on) other operations that it theoretically should also be similar to. For instance, to show the _____ of a test of mathematics skills, the scores on the test can be correlated with scores on other tests that are also designed to measure basic mathematics ability. High correlations between the test scores would be evidence of a _____.
    a. Criterion validity
    b. Content validity
    c. Convergent validity
    d. Discriminant validity

19. _____ is a rivalry between individuals, groups, nations for territory, a niche, or allocation of resources. It arises whenever two or more parties strive for a goal which cannot be shared. _____ occurs naturally between living organisms which co-exist in the same environment.
    a. Non-price competition
    b. Price competition
    c. Competition
    d. Price fixing

20. _____ refer to a collection of facts usually collected as the result of experience, observation or experiment or a set of premises. This may consist of numbers, words particularly as measurements or observations of a set of variables. _____ are often viewed as a lowest level of abstraction from which information and knowledge are derived.
   a. Sample size
   b. Pearson product-moment correlation coefficient
   c. Mean
   d. Data

21. Combining Existing _____ Sources with New Primary Data Sources

Imagine that we could get hold of a good collection of surveys taken in earlier years, such as detailed studies about changes going on in this phase and hopefully additional studies in the years to come. Analyzing this data base over time could give us a good picture of what changes actually have taken place in the orientation of the population and of the extent to which new technical concepts did have an impact on subgroups of the population. Furthermore, data archives can help to prepare studies on change over time by monitoring what questions have been asked in earlier years and alerting principal investigators to important questions which should be repeated in planned research projects.

   a. 180SearchAssistant
   b. 6-3-5 Brainwriting
   c. Secondary Data
   d. Power III

22. A _____ is a research instrument consisting of a series of questions and other prompts for the purpose of gathering information from respondents. Although they are often designed for statistical analysis of the responses, this is not always the case. The _____ was invented by Sir Francis Galton.
   a. Mystery shopping
   b. Mystery shoppers
   c. Market research
   d. Questionnaire

Chapter 11. Sampling Procedures

1. A _____ is a structured collection of records or data that is stored in a computer system. The structure is achieved by organizing the data according to a _____ model. The model in most common use today is the relational model.
   a. 6-3-5 Brainwriting
   b. 180SearchAssistant
   c. Database
   d. Power III

2. _____ is a way of expressing knowledge or belief that an event will occur or has occurred. In mathematics the concept has been given an exact meaning in _____ theory, that is used extensively in such areas of study as mathematics, statistics, finance, gambling, science, and philosophy to draw conclusions about the likelihood of potential events and the underlying mechanics of complex systems.
   a. Heteroskedastic
   b. Linear regression
   c. Data
   d. Probability

3. A sample is a subject chosen from a population for investigation. A _____ is one chosen by a method involving an unpredictable component. Random sampling can also refer to taking a number of independent observations from the same probability distribution, without involving any real population.
   a. 180SearchAssistant
   b. Power III
   c. Selection bias
   d. Random sample

4. The _____ of a statistical sample is the number of observations that constitute it. It is typically denoted n, a positive integer (natural number.)

Typically, all else being equal, a larger _____ leads to increased precision in estimates of various properties of the population.

   a. Heteroskedastic
   b. Frequency distribution
   c. Data
   d. Sample size

5. _____ is that part of statistical practice concerned with the selection of individual observations intended to yield some knowledge about a population of concern, especially for the purposes of statistical inference. Each observation measures one or more properties (weight, location, etc.) of an observable entity enumerated to distinguish objects or individuals.

a. Sports Marketing Group
b. AStore
c. Sampling
d. Richard Buckminster 'Bucky' Fuller

6. _____ is anything that is intended to save time, energy or frustration. A _____ store at a petrol station, for example, sells items that have nothing to do with gasoline/petrol, but it saves the consumer from having to go to a grocery store. '_____' is a very relative term and its meaning tends to change over time.
   a. MaxDiff
   b. Marketing buzz
   c. Convenience
   d. Demographic profile

7. _____s are errors in measurement that lead to measured values being inconsistent when repeated measures of a constant attribute or quantity are taken. The word random indicates that they are inherently unpredictable, and have null expected value, namely, they are scattered about the true value, and tend to have null arithmetic mean when a measurement is repeated several times with the same instrument. All measurements are prone to _____.
   a. Power III
   b. 180SearchAssistant
   c. Systematic error
   d. Random error

8. In statistics, _____ or estimation error is the error caused by observing a sample instead of the whole population.

An estimate of a quantity of interest, such as an average or percentage, will generally be subject to sample-to-sample variation. These variations in the possible sample values of a statistic can theoretically be expressed as _____s, although in practice the exact _____ is typically unknown.

   a. Varimax rotation
   b. Two-tailed test
   c. Sampling error
   d. Power III

9. In statistics, a simple random sample is a subset of individuals (a sample) chosen from a larger set (a population.) Each individual is chosen randomly and entirely by chance, such that each individual has the same probability of being chosen at any stage during the sampling process, and each subset of k individuals has the same probability of being chosen for the sample as any other subset of k individuals (.) This process and technique is known as _____, and should not be confused with Random Sampling.

a. Focus group
b. Logit analysis
c. Market analysis
d. Simple random sampling

10. In mathematics and statistics, the arithmetic mean (or simply the mean) of a list of numbers is the sum of all of the list divided by the number of items in the list. If the list is a statistical population, then the mean of that population is called a population mean. If the list is a statistical sample, we call the resulting statistic a _____.
   a. Null hypothesis
   b. Sample mean
   c. Coefficient of variation
   d. Z-test

11. In statistics, a _____ is an interval estimate of a population parameter. Instead of estimating the parameter by a single value, an interval likely to include the parameter is given. Thus, _____s are used to indicate the reliability of an estimate.
   a. Confidence interval
   b. Linear regression
   c. T-test
   d. Sample mean

12. In statistics, _____ has two related meanings:

   - the arithmetic _____
   - the expected value of a random variable, which is also called the population _____.

It is sometimes stated that the '_____' _____s average. This is incorrect if '_____' is taken in the specific sense of 'arithmetic _____' as there are different types of averages: the _____, median, and mode. For instance, average house prices almost always use the median value for the average. These three types of averages are all measures of locations.

   a. Standard normal distribution
   b. Confidence interval
   c. Heteroskedastic
   d. Mean

Chapter 11. Sampling Procedures

13. In probability theory and statistics, the _____ of a random variable, probability distribution, or sample is a measure of statistical dispersion, averaging the squared distance of its possible values from the expected value (mean.) Whereas the mean is a way to describe the location of a distribution, the _____ is a way to capture its scale or degree of being spread out. The unit of _____ is the square of the unit of the original variable.

   a. Sample size
   b. Correlation
   c. Standard deviation
   d. Variance

14. _____ is one of the four elements of marketing mix. An organization or set of organizations (go-betweens) involved in the process of making a product or service available for use or consumption by a consumer or business user.

The other three parts of the marketing mix are product, pricing, and promotion.

   a. Japan Advertising Photographers' Association
   b. Distribution
   c. Comparison-Shopping agent
   d. Better Living Through Chemistry

15. In statistics, _____ is a method of sampling from a population.

When sub-populations vary considerably, it is advantageous to sample each subpopulation (stratum) independently. Stratification is the process of grouping members of the population into relatively homogeneous subgroups before sampling.

   a. Coefficient of variation
   b. T-test
   c. Data
   d. Stratified sampling

16. _____ is a statistical method involving the selection of elements from an ordered sampling frame. The most common form of _____ is an equal-probability method, in which every k^{th} element in the frame is selected, where k, the sampling interval (sometimes known as the 'skip'), is calculated as:

$$\text{sample size (n)} = \text{population size (N)} / k$$

Using this procedure each element in the population has a known and equal probability of selection. This makes _____ functionally similar to simple random sampling.

a. Systematic sampling
b. 180SearchAssistant
c. Selection bias
d. Power III

Chapter 12. Determining Sample Size

1. The _____ of a statistical sample is the number of observations that constitute it. It is typically denoted n, a positive integer (natural number.)

Typically, all else being equal, a larger _____ leads to increased precision in estimates of various properties of the population.

   a. Sample size
   b. Heteroskedastic
   c. Frequency distribution
   d. Data

2. In statistics, a _____ is an interval estimate of a population parameter. Instead of estimating the parameter by a single value, an interval likely to include the parameter is given. Thus, _____s are used to indicate the reliability of an estimate.
   a. Confidence interval
   b. Sample mean
   c. Linear regression
   d. T-test

3. In mathematics and statistics, the arithmetic mean (or simply the mean) of a list of numbers is the sum of all of the list divided by the number of items in the list. If the list is a statistical population, then the mean of that population is called a population mean. If the list is a statistical sample, we call the resulting statistic a _____.
   a. Coefficient of variation
   b. Z-test
   c. Sample mean
   d. Null hypothesis

4. In statistics, _____ has two related meanings:

   - the arithmetic _____
   - the expected value of a random variable, which is also called the population _____.

It is sometimes stated that the '_____' _____s average. This is incorrect if '_____' is taken in the specific sense of 'arithmetic _____' as there are different types of averages: the _____, median, and mode. For instance, average house prices almost always use the median value for the average. These three types of averages are all measures of locations.

a. Mean
b. Heteroskedastic
c. Standard normal distribution
d. Confidence interval

5. In probability theory and statistics, the _____ of a random variable, probability distribution, or sample is a measure of statistical dispersion, averaging the squared distance of its possible values from the expected value (mean.) Whereas the mean is a way to describe the location of a distribution, the _____ is a way to capture its scale or degree of being spread out. The unit of _____ is the square of the unit of the original variable.
a. Sample size
b. Standard deviation
c. Correlation
d. Variance

6. In economics, business, retail, and accounting, a _____ is the value of money that has been used up to produce something, and hence is not available for use anymore. In economics, a _____ is an alternative that is given up as a result of a decision. In business, the _____ may be one of acquisition, in which case the amount of money expended to acquire it is counted as _____.
a. Transaction cost
b. Fixed costs
c. Variable cost
d. Cost

7. In population genetics and population ecology, _____ is the number of individual organisms in a population.

The effective _____ (N_e) is defined as 'the number of breeding individuals in an idealized population that would show the same amount of dispersion of allele frequencies under random genetic drift or the same amount of inbreeding as the population under consideration.' N_e is usually less than N (the absolute _____) and this has important applications in conservation genetics.

Small _____ results in increased genetic drift.

a. Power III
b. Population size
c. 6-3-5 Brainwriting
d. 180SearchAssistant

Chapter 12. Determining Sample Size

8. _____ refer to a collection of facts usually collected as the result of experience, observation or experiment or a set of premises. This may consist of numbers, words particularly as measurements or observations of a set of variables. _____ are often viewed as a lowest level of abstraction from which information and knowledge are derived.

   a. Pearson product-moment correlation coefficient
   b. Mean
   c. Sample size
   d. Data

9. Combining Existing _____ Sources with New Primary Data Sources

Imagine that we could get hold of a good collection of surveys taken in earlier years, such as detailed studies about changes going on in this phase and hopefully additional studies in the years to come. Analyzing this data base over time could give us a good picture of what changes actually have taken place in the orientation of the population and of the extent to which new technical concepts did have an impact on subgroups of the population. Furthermore, data archives can help to prepare studies on change over time by monitoring what questions have been asked in earlier years and alerting principal investigators to important questions which should be repeated in planned research projects.

   a. Power III
   b. Secondary data
   c. 180SearchAssistant
   d. 6-3-5 Brainwriting

10. _____ is a business term meaning the market segment to which a particular good or service is marketed. It is mainly defined by age, gender, geography, socio-economic grouping, technographic, or any other combination of demographics. It is generally studied and mapped by an organization through lists and reports containing demographic information that may have an effect on the marketing of key products or services.

    a. Brando
    b. Category Development Index
    c. Distribution
    d. Market specialization

Chapter 13. Collecting the Data: Field Procedures and Nonsampling Errors

1. _____ is either an activity of a living being (such as a human), consisting of receiving knowledge of the outside world through the senses, or the recording of data using scientific instruments. The term may also refer to any datum collected during this activity.

The scientific method requires _____s of nature to formulate and test hypotheses.

   a. ADTECH
   b. AMAX
   c. ACNielsen
   d. Observation

2. _____s are errors in measurement that lead to measured values being inconsistent when repeated measures of a constant attribute or quantity are taken. The word random indicates that they are inherently unpredictable, and have null expected value, namely, they are scattered about the true value, and tend to have null arithmetic mean when a measurement is repeated several times with the same instrument. All measurements are prone to _____.
   a. Systematic error
   b. Random error
   c. 180SearchAssistant
   d. Power III

3. _____ is that part of statistical practice concerned with the selection of individual observations intended to yield some knowledge about a population of concern, especially for the purposes of statistical inference. Each observation measures one or more properties (weight, location, etc.) of an observable entity enumerated to distinguish objects or individuals.
   a. Sports Marketing Group
   b. AStore
   c. Sampling
   d. Richard Buckminster 'Bucky' Fuller

4. _____ is a standard point of view or personal prejudice. especially when the tendency interferes with the ability to be impartial, unprejudiced, or objective. The term _____ed is used to describe an action, judgment, or other outcome influenced by a prejudged perspective.
   a. 6-3-5 Brainwriting
   b. 180SearchAssistant
   c. Power III
   d. Bias

Chapter 13. Collecting the Data: Field Procedures and Nonsampling Errors

5. An _____ is a special-purpose computer system designed to perform one or a few dedicated functions, often with real-time computing constraints. It is usually embedded as part of a complete device including hardware and mechanical parts. In contrast, a general-purpose computer, such as a personal computer, can do many different tasks depending on programming.
   a. ADTECH
   b. ACNielsen
   c. AMAX
   d. Embedded system

6. _____ is the practice of individuals including commercial businesses, governments and institutions, facilitating the sale of their products or services to other companies or organizations that in turn resell them, use them as components in products or services they offer _____ is also called business-to-_____ for short. (Note that while marketing to government entities shares some of the same dynamics of organizational marketing, B2G Marketing is meaningfully different.)
   a. Law of disruption
   b. Mass marketing
   c. Disruptive technology
   d. Business marketing

7. _____ a research method involving the use of questionnaires and/or statistical surveys to gather data about people and their thoughts and behaviours.
   a. Survey Research
   b. T-test
   c. Z-test
   d. Control chart

8. _____ in survey research refers to the ratio of number of people who answered the survey divided by the number of people in the sample. It is usually expressed in the form of a percentage.

Example: if 1,000 surveys were sent by mail, and 257 were successfully completed and returned, then the _____ would be 25.7 %.

   a. Reference value
   b. Sentence completion tests
   c. Power III
   d. Response rate

Chapter 13. Collecting the Data: Field Procedures and Nonsampling Errors

9. In calculus, a function f defined on a subset of the real numbers with real values is called _____, if for all x and y such that x ≤ y one has f(x) ≤ f(y), so f preserves the order. In layman's terms, the sign of the slope is always positive (the curve tending upwards) or zero (i.e., non-decreasing, or asymptotic, or depicted as a horizontal, flat line) Likewise, a function is called monotonically decreasing (non-increasing) if, whenever x ≤ y, then f(x) ≥ f(y), so it reverses the order.
    a. 6-3-5 Brainwriting
    b. 180SearchAssistant
    c. Power III
    d. Monotonic

10. In statistics, an _____ is a term in a statistical model added when the effect of two or more variables is not simply additive. Such a term reflects that the effect of one variable depends on the values of one or more other variables.

    Thus, for a response Y and two variables x_1 and x_2 an additive model would be:

    $$Y = ax_1 + bx_2 + \text{error}$$

    In contrast to this,

    $$Y = ax_1 + bx_2 + c(x_1 \times x_2) + \text{error},$$

    is an example of a model with an _____ between variables x_1 and x_2 ('error' refers to the random variable whose value by which y differs from the expected value of y.)

    a. ADTECH
    b. AMAX
    c. ACNielsen
    d. Interaction

11. The _____ is a professional association for marketers. As of 2008 it had approximately 40,000 members. There are collegiate chapters on 250 campuses.
    a. ACNielsen
    b. ADTECH
    c. AMAX
    d. American Marketing Association

12. _____ is defined by the American _____ Association as the activity, set of institutions, and processes for creating, communicating, delivering, and exchanging offerings that have value for customers, clients, partners, and society at large. The term developed from the original meaning which referred literally to going to market, as in shopping, or going to a market to sell goods or services.

_____ practice tends to be seen as a creative industry, which includes advertising, distribution and selling.

a. Customer acquisition management
b. Marketing myopia
c. Product naming
d. Marketing

13. Consumer market research is a form of applied sociology that concentrates on understanding the behaviours, whims and preferences, of consumers in a market-based economy, and aims to understand the effects and comparative success of marketing campaigns. The field of consumer _____ as a statistical science was pioneered by Arthur Nielsen with the founding of the ACNielsen Company in 1923 .

Thus _____ is the systematic and objective identification, collection, analysis, and dissemination of information for the purpose of assisting management in decision making related to the identification and solution of problems and opportunities in marketing.

a. Focus group
b. Marketing research process
c. Logit analysis
d. Marketing research

14. In environmental modeling and especially in hydrology, a _____ model means a model that is acceptably consistent with observed natural processes, i.e. that simulates well, for example, observed river discharge. It is a key concept of the so-called Generalized Likelihood Uncertainty Estimation (GLUE) methodology to quantify how uncertain environmental predictions are.
a. Power III
b. 180SearchAssistant
c. 6-3-5 Brainwriting
d. Behavioral

15. In economics, business, retail, and accounting, a _____ is the value of money that has been used up to produce something, and hence is not available for use anymore. In economics, a _____ is an alternative that is given up as a result of a decision. In business, the _____ may be one of acquisition, in which case the amount of money expended to acquire it is counted as _____ .

a. Fixed costs
b. Cost
c. Variable cost
d. Transaction cost

16. _____ refer to a collection of facts usually collected as the result of experience, observation or experiment or a set of premises. This may consist of numbers, words particularly as measurements or observations of a set of variables. _____ are often viewed as a lowest level of abstraction from which information and knowledge are derived.
   a. Mean
   b. Pearson product-moment correlation coefficient
   c. Sample size
   d. Data

17. The _____ is the official currency of 16 out of 27 member states of the European Union (EU.) The states, known collectively as the Eurozone are: Austria, Belgium, Cyprus, Finland, France, Germany, Greece, Ireland, Italy, Luxembourg, Malta, the Netherlands, Portugal, Slovakia, Slovenia, and Spain. The currency is also used in a further five European countries, with and without formal agreements and is consequently used daily by some 327 million Europeans.
   a. Euro
   b. Eurozone
   c. ACNielsen
   d. ADTECH

Chapter 14. Preprocessing the Data, and Doing Cross-Tabs

1. _____ refer to a collection of facts usually collected as the result of experience, observation or experiment or a set of premises. This may consist of numbers, words particularly as measurements or observations of a set of variables. _____ are often viewed as a lowest level of abstraction from which information and knowledge are derived.
   a. Data
   b. Pearson product-moment correlation coefficient
   c. Sample size
   d. Mean

2. _____ is a process of gathering, modeling, and transforming data with the goal of highlighting useful information, suggesting conclusions, and supporting decision making. _____ has multiple facets and approaches, encompassing diverse techniques under a variety of names, in different business, science, and social science domains.

   Data mining is a particular _____ technique that focuses on modeling and knowledge discovery for predictive rather than purely descriptive purposes.

   a. Power III
   b. 180SearchAssistant
   c. 6-3-5 Brainwriting
   d. Data analysis

3. A _____ displays the joint distribution of two or more variables. They are usually presented as a contingency table in a matrix format. Whereas a frequency distribution provides the distribution of one variable, a contingency table describes the distribution of two or more variables simultaneously.
   a. Cross Tabulation
   b. Logit analysis
   c. Marketing research
   d. Marketing research process

4. _____ is one of the four elements of marketing mix. An organization or set of organizations (go-betweens) involved in the process of making a product or service available for use or consumption by a consumer or business user.

   The other three parts of the marketing mix are product, pricing, and promotion.

   a. Comparison-Shopping agent
   b. Distribution
   c. Japan Advertising Photographers' Association
   d. Better Living Through Chemistry

Chapter 14. Preprocessing the Data, and Doing Cross-Tabs   81

5. A _____ is any statistical hypothesis test in which the test statistic has a chi-square distribution when the null hypothesis is true, or any in which the probability distribution of the test statistic (assuming the null hypothesis is true) can be made to approximate a chi-square distribution as closely as desired by making the sample size large enough.

Some examples of chi-squared tests where the chi-square distribution is only approximately valid:

- Pearson's _____, also known as the chi-square goodness-of-fit test or _____ for independence. When mentioned without any modifiers or without other precluding context, this test is usually understood.
- Yates' _____, also known as Yates' correction for continuity.
- Mantel-Haenszel _____.
- Linear-by-linear association _____.
- The portmanteau test in time-series analysis, testing for the presence of autocorrelation
- Likelihood-ratio tests in general statistical modelling, for testing whether there is evidence of the need to move from a simple model to a more complicated one (where the simple model is nested within the complicated one.)

One case where the distribution of the test statistic is an exact chi-square distribution is the test that the variance of a normally-distributed population has a given value based on a sample variance. Such a test is uncommon in practice because values of variances to test against are seldom known exactly.

If a sample of size n is taken from a population having a normal distribution, then there is a well-known result which allows a test to be made of whether the variance of the population has a pre-determined value.

a. Type I error
b. Confounding variables
c. Randomization
d. Chi-square test

6. _____s are used in open sentences. For instance, in the formula x + 1 = 5, x is a _____ which represents an 'unknown' number. _____s are often represented by letters of the Roman alphabet, or those of other alphabets, such as Greek, and use other special symbols.
a. Variable
b. Personalization
c. Book of business
d. Quantitative

7. _____ is a way of expressing knowledge or belief that an event will occur or has occurred. In mathematics the concept has been given an exact meaning in _____ theory, that is used extensively in such areas of study as mathematics, statistics, finance, gambling, science, and philosophy to draw conclusions about the likelihood of potential events and the underlying mechanics of complex systems.

Chapter 14. Preprocessing the Data, and Doing Cross-Tabs

a. Data
b. Linear regression
c. Heteroskedastic
d. Probability

8. In statistics, a _____ is a mathematical relationship in which two occurrences have no causal connection, yet it may be inferred that they do, due to a certain third, unseen factor (referred to as a 'confounding factor' or 'lurking variable'.) The _____ gives an impression of a worthy link between two groups that is invalid when objectively examined.

The misleading correlation between two variables is produced through the operation of a third causal variable.

a. 180SearchAssistant
b. 6-3-5 Brainwriting
c. Spurious relationship
d. Power III

9. In probability theory and statistics, _____ indicates the strength and direction of a linear relationship between two random variables. That is in contrast with the usage of the term in colloquial speech, denoting any relationship, not necessarily linear. In general statistical usage, _____ or co-relation refers to the departure of two random variables from independence.

a. Correlation
b. Mean
c. Probability
d. Frequency distribution

10. In statistical hypothesis testing, the _____ formally describes some aspect of the statistical behaviour of a set of data; this description is treated as valid unless the actual behaviour of the data contradicts this assumption. Thus, the _____ is contrasted against another hypothesis. Statistical hypothesis testing is used to make a decision about whether the data contradicts the _____: this is called significance testing.

a. Variance
b. Standard score
c. Null hypothesis
d. Statistical hypothesis test

11. A _____ is a statement or claim that a particular event will occur in the future in more certain terms than a forecast. The etymology of this word is Latin . In regards to predicting the future Howard H. Stevenson Says, ' _____ is at least two things: Important and hard.' Important, because we have to act, and hard because we have to realize the future we want, and what is the best way to get there.

a. Power III
b. 180SearchAssistant
c. 6-3-5 Brainwriting
d. Prediction

Chapter 15. Data Analysis—Basic Questions

1. _____ refer to a collection of facts usually collected as the result of experience, observation or experiment or a set of premises. This may consist of numbers, words particularly as measurements or observations of a set of variables. _____ are often viewed as a lowest level of abstraction from which information and knowledge are derived.

   a. Data
   b. Sample size
   c. Pearson product-moment correlation coefficient
   d. Mean

2. _____ is a process of gathering, modeling, and transforming data with the goal of highlighting useful information, suggesting conclusions, and supporting decision making. _____ has multiple facets and approaches, encompassing diverse techniques under a variety of names, in different business, science, and social science domains.

Data mining is a particular _____ technique that focuses on modeling and knowledge discovery for predictive rather than purely descriptive purposes.

   a. 180SearchAssistant
   b. Power III
   c. 6-3-5 Brainwriting
   d. Data analysis

3. A _____ is any statistical hypothesis test in which the test statistic has a chi-square distribution when the null hypothesis is true, or any in which the probability distribution of the test statistic (assuming the null hypothesis is true) can be made to approximate a chi-square distribution as closely as desired by making the sample size large enough.

Some examples of chi-squared tests where the chi-square distribution is only approximately valid:

   - Pearson's _____, also known as the chi-square goodness-of-fit test or _____ for independence. When mentioned without any modifiers or without other precluding context, this test is usually understood.
   - Yates' _____, also known as Yates' correction for continuity.
   - Mantel-Haenszel _____.
   - Linear-by-linear association _____.
   - The portmanteau test in time-series analysis, testing for the presence of autocorrelation
   - Likelihood-ratio tests in general statistical modelling, for testing whether there is evidence of the need to move from a simple model to a more complicated one (where the simple model is nested within the complicated one.)

One case where the distribution of the test statistic is an exact chi-square distribution is the test that the variance of a normally-distributed population has a given value based on a sample variance. Such a test is uncommon in practice because values of variances to test against are seldom known exactly.

If a sample of size n is taken from a population having a normal distribution, then there is a well-known result which allows a test to be made of whether the variance of the population has a pre-determined value.

a. Confounding variables
b. Type I error
c. Randomization
d. Chi-square test

4. The '_____' is an expression which typically refers to the theory of scale types developed by the Harvard psychologist Stanley Smith Stevens In this article Stevens claimed that all measurement in science was conducted using four different types of numerical scales which he called 'nominal', 'ordinal', 'interval' and 'ratio'.
   a. 180SearchAssistant
   b. Power III
   c. 6-3-5 Brainwriting
   d. Levels of measurement

5. In probability theory and statistics, a _____ is described as the number separating the higher half of a sample, a population from the lower half. The _____ of a finite list of numbers can be found by arranging all the observations from lowest value to highest value and picking the middle one. If there is an even number of observations, the _____ is not unique, so one often takes the mean of the two middle values.
   a. Frequency distribution
   b. Statistically significant
   c. Linear regression
   d. Median

6. In algebra, the _____ of a polynomial with real or complex coefficients is a certain expression in the coefficients of the polynomial which is equal to zero if and only if the polynomial has a multiple root (i.e. a root with multiplicity greater than one) in the complex numbers. For example, the _____ of the quadratic polynomial

$$ax^2 + bx + c \text{ is } b^2 - 4ac.$$

The _____ of the cubic polynomial

$$ax^3 + bx^2 + cx + d \text{ is } b^2c^2 - 4ac^3 - 4b^3d - 27a^2d^2 + 18abcd.$$

a. Flighting
b. Consumption Map
c. Lifestyle center
d. Discriminant

7. _____ describes the degree to which the operationalization is not similar to (diverges from) other operationalizations that it theoretically should not be similar to.

Campbell and Fiske (1959) introduced the concept of _____ within their discussion on evaluating test validity. They stressed the importance of using both discriminant and convergent validation techniques when assessing new tests.

a. Convergent validity
b. Predictive validity
c. Criterion validity
d. Discriminant validity

8. A number of different _____s are indicated below.

- Randomized controlled trial
    o Double-blind randomized trial
    o Single-blind randomized trial
    o Non-blind trial
- Nonrandomized trial (quasi-experiment)
    o Interrupted time series design (measures on a sample or a series of samples from the same population are obtained several times before and after a manipulated event or a naturally occurring event) - considered a type of quasi-experiment
- Cohort study
    o Prospective cohort
    o Retrospective cohort
    o Time series study
- Case-control study
    o Nested case-control study
- Cross-sectional study
    o Community survey (a type of cross-sectional study)

When choosing a _____, many factors must be taken into account. Different types of studies are subject to different types of bias. For example, recall bias is likely to occur in cross-sectional or case-control studies where subjects are asked to recall exposure to risk factors.

a. 180SearchAssistant
b. Longitudinal studies
c. Power III
d. Study design

9. _____s are used in open sentences. For instance, in the formula x + 1 = 5, x is a _____ which represents an 'unknown' number. _____s are often represented by letters of the Roman alphabet, or those of other alphabets, such as Greek, and use other special symbols.
   a. Book of business
   b. Quantitative
   c. Variable
   d. Personalization

10. _____ is a mathematical science pertaining to the collection, analysis, interpretation or explanation, and presentation of data. It also provides tools for prediction and forecasting based on data. It is applicable to a wide variety of academic disciplines, from the natural and social sciences to the humanities, government and business.
    a. Type I error
    b. Null hypothesis
    c. Median
    d. Statistics

11. In statistical hypothesis testing, the _____ formally describes some aspect of the statistical behaviour of a set of data; this description is treated as valid unless the actual behaviour of the data contradicts this assumption. Thus, the _____ is contrasted against another hypothesis. Statistical hypothesis testing is used to make a decision about whether the data contradicts the _____: this is called significance testing.
    a. Statistical hypothesis test
    b. Standard score
    c. Null hypothesis
    d. Variance

Chapter 16. Are My Groups the Same or Different?

1. In statistics, _____ has two related meanings:

    - the arithmetic _____
    - the expected value of a random variable, which is also called the population _____.

It is sometimes stated that the '_____' _____s average. This is incorrect if '_____' is taken in the specific sense of 'arithmetic _____' as there are different types of averages: the _____, median, and mode. For instance, average house prices almost always use the median value for the average. These three types of averages are all measures of locations.

   a. Confidence interval
   b. Standard normal distribution
   c. Heteroskedastic
   d. Mean

2. In statistical hypothesis testing, the _____ formally describes some aspect of the statistical behaviour of a set of data; this description is treated as valid unless the actual behaviour of the data contradicts this assumption. Thus, the _____ is contrasted against another hypothesis. Statistical hypothesis testing is used to make a decision about whether the data contradicts the _____: this is called significance testing.
   a. Null hypothesis
   b. Variance
   c. Standard score
   d. Statistical hypothesis test

3. In probability theory and statistics, the _____ of a random variable, probability distribution, or sample is a measure of statistical dispersion, averaging the squared distance of its possible values from the expected value (mean.) Whereas the mean is a way to describe the location of a distribution, the _____ is a way to capture its scale or degree of being spread out. The unit of _____ is the square of the unit of the original variable.
   a. Correlation
   b. Standard deviation
   c. Sample size
   d. Variance

4. In economics, business, retail, and accounting, a _____ is the value of money that has been used up to produce something, and hence is not available for use anymore. In economics, a _____ is an alternative that is given up as a result of a decision. In business, the _____ may be one of acquisition, in which case the amount of money expended to acquire it is counted as _____.

a. Transaction cost
b. Fixed costs
c. Variable cost
d. Cost

5. _____ refer to a collection of facts usually collected as the result of experience, observation or experiment or a set of premises. This may consist of numbers, words particularly as measurements or observations of a set of variables. _____ are often viewed as a lowest level of abstraction from which information and knowledge are derived.

a. Sample size
b. Mean
c. Pearson product-moment correlation coefficient
d. Data

6. _____ is defined by the American _____ Association as the activity, set of institutions, and processes for creating, communicating, delivering, and exchanging offerings that have value for customers, clients, partners, and society at large. The term developed from the original meaning which referred literally to going to market, as in shopping, or going to a market to sell goods or services.

_____ practice tends to be seen as a creative industry, which includes advertising, distribution and selling.

a. Marketing
b. Product naming
c. Customer acquisition management
d. Marketing myopia

7. Consumer market research is a form of applied sociology that concentrates on understanding the behaviours, whims and preferences, of consumers in a market-based economy, and aims to understand the effects and comparative success of marketing campaigns. The field of consumer _____ as a statistical science was pioneered by Arthur Nielsen with the founding of the ACNielsen Company in 1923.

Thus _____ is the systematic and objective identification, collection, analysis, and dissemination of information for the purpose of assisting management in decision making related to the identification and solution of problems and opportunities in marketing.

a. Logit analysis
b. Focus group
c. Marketing research
d. Marketing research process

Chapter 16. Are My Groups the Same or Different?

8. A _____ is the space, actual or metaphorical, in which a market operates. The term is also used in a trademark law context to denote the actual consumer environment, ie. the 'real world' in which products and services are provided and consumed.
   a. 180SearchAssistant
   b. 6-3-5 Brainwriting
   c. Power III
   d. Marketplace

9. _____ is a statistical method used to describe variability among observed variables in terms of fewer unobserved variables called factors. The observed variables are modeled as linear combinations of the factors, plus 'error' terms. The information gained about the interdependencies can be used later to reduce the set of variables in a dataset.
   a. Likert scale
   b. Power III
   c. Semantic differential
   d. Factor analysis

10. In the design of experiments, _____ are for studying the effects of one primary factor without the need to take other nuisance factors into account The experiment compares the values of a response variable based on the different levels of that primary factor.
    a. Comprehensive,
    b. Just-In-Case
    c. Geo
    d. Completely randomized designs

Chapter 17. Are These Variables Related?

1. The terms '_____' and 'independent variable' are used in similar but subtly different ways in mathematics and statistics as part of the standard terminology in those subjects. They are used to distinguish between two types of quantities being considered, separating them into those available at the start of a process and those being created by it, where the latter (_____s) are dependent on the former (independent variables.)

In traditional calculus, a function is defined as a relation between two terms called variables because their values vary.

   a. Power III
   b. Field experiment
   c. 180SearchAssistant
   d. Dependent variable

2. _____ is the process of estimation in unknown situations. Prediction is a similar, but more general term. Both can refer to estimation of time series, cross-sectional or longitudinal data.
   a. 180SearchAssistant
   b. 6-3-5 Brainwriting
   c. Power III
   d. Forecasting

3. A _____ is a statement or claim that a particular event will occur in the future in more certain terms than a forecast. The etymology of this word is Latin . In regards to predicting the future Howard H. Stevenson Says, ' _____ is at least two things: Important and hard.' Important, because we have to act, and hard because we have to realize the future we want, and what is the best way to get there.
   a. Prediction
   b. 6-3-5 Brainwriting
   c. Power III
   d. 180SearchAssistant

4. A _____ is any statistical hypothesis test in which the test statistic has a chi-square distribution when the null hypothesis is true, or any in which the probability distribution of the test statistic (assuming the null hypothesis is true) can be made to approximate a chi-square distribution as closely as desired by making the sample size large enough.

Some examples of chi-squared tests where the chi-square distribution is only approximately valid:

- Pearson's _____, also known as the chi-square goodness-of-fit test or _____ for independence. When mentioned without any modifiers or without other precluding context, this test is usually understood.
- Yates' _____, also known as Yates' correction for continuity.
- Mantel-Haenszel _____.
- Linear-by-linear association _____.
- The portmanteau test in time-series analysis, testing for the presence of autocorrelation
- Likelihood-ratio tests in general statistical modelling, for testing whether there is evidence of the need to move from a simple model to a more complicated one (where the simple model is nested within the complicated one.)

One case where the distribution of the test statistic is an exact chi-square distribution is the test that the variance of a normally-distributed population has a given value based on a sample variance. Such a test is uncommon in practice because values of variances to test against are seldom known exactly.

If a sample of size n is taken from a population having a normal distribution, then there is a well-known result which allows a test to be made of whether the variance of the population has a pre-determined value.

a. Randomization
b. Type I error
c. Confounding variables
d. Chi-square test

5. _____ are variables other than the independent variable that may bear any effect on the behavior of the subject being studied.

_____ are often classified into three main types:

1. Subject variables, which are the characteristics of the individuals being studied that might affect their actions. These variables include age, gender, health status, mood, background, etc.
2. Experimental variables are characteristics of the persons conducting the experiment which might influence how a person behaves. Gender, the presence of racial discrimination, language, or other factors may qualify as such variables.
3. Situational variables are features of the environment in which the study or research was conducted, which have a bearing on the outcome of the experiment in a negative way. Included are the air temperature, level of activity, lighting, and the time of day.

There are two strategies of controlling _____. Either a potentially influential variable is kept the same for all subjects in the research, or they balance the variables in a group.

Chapter 17. Are These Variables Related?

Take for example an experiment, in which a salesperson sells clothing on a door-to-door basis.

a. ACNielsen
b. AMAX
c. Extraneous variables
d. ADTECH

6. _____s are used in open sentences. For instance, in the formula x + 1 = 5, x is a _____ which represents an 'unknown' number. _____s are often represented by letters of the Roman alphabet, or those of other alphabets, such as Greek, and use other special symbols.
   a. Book of business
   b. Personalization
   c. Variable
   d. Quantitative

7. In probability theory and statistics, _____ indicates the strength and direction of a linear relationship between two random variables. That is in contrast with the usage of the term in colloquial speech, denoting any relationship, not necessarily linear. In general statistical usage, _____ or co-relation refers to the departure of two random variables from independence.
   a. Frequency distribution
   b. Probability
   c. Mean
   d. Correlation

8. In statistics, _____ is a collective name for techniques for the modeling and analysis of numerical data consisting of values of a dependent variable and of one or more independent variables The dependent variable in the regression equation is modeled as a function of the independent variables, corresponding parameters, and an error term. The error term is treated as a random variable.
   a. Multicollinearity
   b. Regression analysis
   c. Stepwise regression
   d. Variance inflation factor

9. _____ refer to a collection of facts usually collected as the result of experience, observation or experiment or a set of premises. This may consist of numbers, words particularly as measurements or observations of a set of variables. _____ are often viewed as a lowest level of abstraction from which information and knowledge are derived.

a. Mean
b. Pearson product-moment correlation coefficient
c. Sample size
d. Data

10. In statistics, _____ is used for two things;

- to construct a simple formula that will predict what value will occur for a quantity of interest when other related variables take given values.
- to allow a test to be made of whether a given variable does have an effect on a quantity of interest in situations where there may be many related variables.

In both cases, several sets of outcomes are available for the quantity of interest together with the related variables.

_____ is a form of regression analysis in which the relationship between one or more independent variables and another variable, called the dependent variable, is modelled by a least squares function, called a _____ equation. This function is a linear combination of one or more model parameters, called regression coefficients. A _____ equation with one independent variable represents a straight line when the predicted value (i.e. the dependant variable from the regression equation) is plotted against the independent variable: this is called a simple _____.

a. Descriptive statistics
b. Heteroskedastic
c. Linear regression
d. Sample size

11. In statistics, the _____, R^2 is used in the context of statistical models whose main purpose is the prediction of future outcomes on the basis of other related information. It is the proportion of variability in a data set that is accounted for by the statistical model. It provides a measure of how well future outcomes are likely to be predicted by the model.
a. Coefficient of determination
b. Variance inflation factor
c. Multicollinearity
d. Regression analysis

12. _____ is a statistical phenomenon in which two or more predictor variables in a multiple regression model are highly correlated. In this situation the coefficient estimates may change erratically in response to small changes in the model or the data. _____ does not reduce the predictive power or reliability of the model as a whole; it only affects calculations regarding individual predictors.

a. Multicollinearity
b. Variance inflation factor
c. Regression analysis
d. Stepwise regression

13. _____ is a statistical technique used in market research to determine how people value different features that make up an individual product or service.

The objective of _____ is to determine what combination of a limited number of attributes is most influential on respondent choice or decision making. A controlled set of potential products or services is shown to respondents and by analyzing how they make preferences between these products, the implicit valuation of the individual elements making up the product or service can be determined.

a. Semantic differential
b. Power III
c. Conjoint analysis
d. Likert scale

14. _____ is a broad label that refers to any individuals or households that use goods and services generated within the economy. The concept of a _____ is used in different contexts, so that the usage and significance of the term may vary.

A _____ is a person who uses any product or service.

a. 6-3-5 Brainwriting
b. Power III
c. Consumer
d. 180SearchAssistant

Chapter 18. Multivariate Data Analysis

1. In algebra, the _____ of a polynomial with real or complex coefficients is a certain expression in the coefficients of the polynomial which is equal to zero if and only if the polynomial has a multiple root (i.e. a root with multiplicity greater than one) in the complex numbers. For example, the _____ of the quadratic polynomial

$$ax^2 + bx + c \text{ is } b^2 - 4ac.$$

The _____ of the cubic polynomial

$$ax^3 + bx^2 + cx + d \text{ is } b^2c^2 - 4ac^3 - 4b^3d - 27a^2d^2 + 18abcd.$$

   a. Lifestyle center
   b. Discriminant
   c. Flighting
   d. Consumption Map

2. Linear _____ and the related Fisher's linear discriminant are methods used in statistics and machine learning to find the linear combination of features which best separate two or more classes of objects or events. The resulting combination may be used as a linear classifier, or, more commonly, for dimensionality reduction before later classification.

LDiscriminant analysis is closely related to ANOVA (analysis of variance) and regression analysis, which also attempt to express one dependent variable as a linear combination of other features or measurements.

   a. Multiple discriminant analysis
   b. Geodemographic segmentation
   c. Discriminant analysis
   d. Linear discriminant analysis

3. _____s are used in open sentences. For instance, in the formula x + 1 = 5, x is a _____ which represents an 'unknown' number. _____s are often represented by letters of the Roman alphabet, or those of other alphabets, such as Greek, and use other special symbols.
   a. Book of business
   b. Quantitative
   c. Personalization
   d. Variable

4. _____ is a statistical method used to describe variability among observed variables in terms of fewer unobserved variables called factors. The observed variables are modeled as linear combinations of the factors, plus 'error' terms. The information gained about the interdependencies can be used later to reduce the set of variables in a dataset.

a. Likert scale
b. Power III
c. Factor analysis
d. Semantic differential

5. _____ is defined by the American _____ Association as the activity, set of institutions, and processes for creating, communicating, delivering, and exchanging offerings that have value for customers, clients, partners, and society at large. The term developed from the original meaning which referred literally to going to market, as in shopping, or going to a market to sell goods or services.

_____ practice tends to be seen as a creative industry, which includes advertising, distribution and selling.

a. Marketing
b. Customer acquisition management
c. Product naming
d. Marketing myopia

6. _____ refer to a collection of facts usually collected as the result of experience, observation or experiment or a set of premises. This may consist of numbers, words particularly as measurements or observations of a set of variables. _____ are often viewed as a lowest level of abstraction from which information and knowledge are derived.

a. Mean
b. Sample size
c. Pearson product-moment correlation coefficient
d. Data

7. '_____' is a class of statistical techniques that can be applied to data that exhibit 'natural' groupings. _____ sorts through the raw data and groups them into clusters. A cluster is a group of relatively homogeneous cases or observations.

a. 180SearchAssistant
b. Power III
c. Structure mining
d. Cluster analysis

8. In mathematics, the _____ or Euclidean metric is the 'ordinary' distance between two points that one would measure with a ruler, which can be proven by repeated application of the Pythagorean theorem. By using this formula as distance, Euclidean space becomes a metric space (even a Hilbert space.) The associated norm is called the Euclidean norm.

a. Euclidean distance
b. AMAX
c. ACNielsen
d. ADTECH

9. _____ is the assignment of objects into groups (called clusters) so that objects from the same cluster are more similar to each other than objects from different clusters. Often similarity is assessed according to a distance measure. _____ is a common technique for statistical data analysis, which is used in many fields, including machine learning, data mining, pattern recognition, image analysis and bioinformatics.
   a. Developed country
   b. Comparison-Shopping agent
   c. Just-In-Case
   d. Clustering

10. In mathematics, an _____, or central tendency of a data set refers to a measure of the 'middle' or 'expected' value of the data set. There are many different descriptive statistics that can be chosen as a measurement of the central tendency of the data items.

An _____ is a single value that is meant to typify a list of values.

   a. ADTECH
   b. ACNielsen
   c. AMAX
   d. Average

11. In genetics _____ is defined as the state in which two loci are so close together that alleles of these loci are virtually never separated by crossing over. During reproduction, chromosomes on the same chromosome pair, exchange sections of DNA. As a result, genes that were originally on the same chromosome can finish up on different chromosomes - genetic recombination.
   a. F-statistics
   b. Complete linkage
   c. 180SearchAssistant
   d. Power III

12. In the mathematical discipline of graph theory a _____ or edge-independent set in a graph is a set of edges without common vertices. It may also be an entire graph consisting of edges without common vertices.

Chapter 18. Multivariate Data Analysis

Given a graph G = (V,E), a _____ M in G is a set of pairwise non-adjacent edges; that is, no two edges share a common vertex.

a. Power III
b. 6-3-5 Brainwriting
c. 180SearchAssistant
d. Matching

13. A personal and cultural _____ is a relative ethic _____, an assumption upon which implementation can be extrapolated. A _____ system is a set of consistent _____s and measures that is soo not true. A principle _____ is a foundation upon which other _____s and measures of integrity are based.

a. Value
b. Package-on-Package
c. Supreme Court of the United States
d. Perceptual maps

14. _____ is a set of related statistical techniques often used in information visualization for exploring similarities or dissimilarities in data. MDS is a special case of ordination. An MDS algorithm starts with a matrix of item-item similarities, then assigns a location to each item in N-dimensional space, where N is specified a priori.

a. Convenience
b. Cocooning
c. Situational theory of publics
d. Multidimensional scaling

15. Perceptual mapping is a graphics technique used by asset marketers that attempts to visually display the perceptions of customers or potential customers. Typically the position of a product, product line, brand, or company is displayed relative to their competition.

_____ can have any number of dimensions but the most common is two dimensions.

a. Developed country
b. Comparison-Shopping agent
c. Retail floor planning
d. Perceptual maps

Chapter 18. Multivariate Data Analysis

16. In the Northern Hemisphere, the _____ or (winter) holiday season (mainly in North American usage) is a late-year season that surrounds the Christmas holiday as well as other holidays during the November/December timeframe. It is sometimes synonymous with the winter season. It has been found to have a proportionate effect on health, compared to the rest of the year.
    a. Christmas season
    b. Power III
    c. 180SearchAssistant
    d. Christmas creep

17. _____ is a multivariate statistical technique developed by Jean-Paul Benzécri that is conceptually similar to principal components analysis, but scales the data (which must be positive) so that rows and columns are treated equivalently. It is traditionally applied to contingency tables. _____ decomposes the Chi-square statistic associated to this table into orthogonal factors.
    a. Correspondence Analysis
    b. Principal component analysis
    c. Geodemographic segmentation
    d. Discriminant analysis

18. An _____ is a special-purpose computer system designed to perform one or a few dedicated functions, often with real-time computing constraints. It is usually embedded as part of a complete device including hardware and mechanical parts. In contrast, a general-purpose computer, such as a personal computer, can do many different tasks depending on programming.
    a. ACNielsen
    b. ADTECH
    c. AMAX
    d. Embedded system

19. Traditionally, the term _____ had been used to refer to a network or circuit of biological neurons. The modern usage of the term often refers to artificial _____s, which are composed of artificial neurons or nodes. Thus the term has two distinct usages:

    1. Biological _____s are made up of real biological neurons that are connected or functionally related in the peripheral nervous system or the central nervous system. In the field of neuroscience, they are often identified as groups of neurons that perform a specific physiological function in laboratory analysis.
    2. Artificial _____s are made up of interconnecting artificial neurons (programming constructs that mimic the properties of biological neurons.) Artificial _____s may either be used to gain an understanding of biological _____s, or for solving artificial intelligence problems without necessarily creating a model of a real biological system. The real, biological nervous system is highly complex and includes some features that may seem superfluous based on an understanding of artificial networks

In general a biological _____ is composed of a group or groups of chemically connected or functionally associated neurons.

a. 6-3-5 Brainwriting
b. Power III
c. Neural network
d. 180SearchAssistant

20. _____ is a form of communication that typically attempts to persuade potential customers to purchase or to consume more of a particular brand of product or service. 'While now central to the contemporary global economy and the reproduction of global production networks, it is only quite recently that _____ has been more than a marginal influence on patterns of sales and production. The formation of modern _____ was intimately bound up with the emergence of new forms of monopoly capitalism around the end of the 19th and beginning of the 20th century as one element in corporate strategies to create, organize and where possible control markets, especially for mass produced consumer goods.
a. AMAX
b. Advertising
c. ADTECH
d. ACNielsen

21. _____ is a rivalry between individuals, groups, nations for territory, a niche, or allocation of resources. It arises whenever two or more parties strive for a goal which cannot be shared. _____ occurs naturally between living organisms which co-exist in the same environment.
a. Competition
b. Price fixing
c. Non-price competition
d. Price competition

22. _____ was originally coined by Austrian psychologist Alfred Adler in 1929. The current broader sense of the word dates from 1961.

In sociology, a _____ is the way a person lives.

a. 6-3-5 Brainwriting
b. Lifestyle
c. Power III
d. 180SearchAssistant

23. _____, a business term, is a measure of how products and services supplied by a company meet or surpass customer expectation. It is seen as a key performance indicator within business and is part of the four perspectives of a Balanced Scorecard.

In a competitive marketplace where businesses compete for customers, _____ is seen as a key differentiator and increasingly has become a key element of business strategy.

   a. Customer base
   b. Supplier diversity
   c. Psychological pricing
   d. Customer Satisfaction

24. A _____ is a collection of symbols, experiences and associations connected with a product, a service, a person or any other artifact or entity.

_____s have become increasingly important components of culture and the economy, now being described as 'cultural accessories and personal philosophies'.

Some people distinguish the psychological aspect of a _____ from the experiential aspect.

   a. Store brand
   b. Brandable software
   c. Brand equity
   d. Brand

Chapter 19. The Research Report

1. _____ is a term used in business for a short document that summarises a longer report, proposal or group of related reports in such a way that readers can rapidly become acquainted with a large body of material without having to read it all. It will usually contain a brief statement of the problem or proposal covered in the major document(s), background information, concise analysis and main conclusions. It is intended as an aid to decision making by business managers.
   a. ADTECH
   b. ACNielsen
   c. AMAX
   d. Executive summary

2. _____ is the process of comparing the cost, cycle time, productivity, or quality of a specific process or method to another that is widely considered to be an industry standard or best practice. The result is often a business case for making changes in order to make improvements. The term _____ was first used by cobblers to measure ones feet for shoes.
   a. Business strategy
   b. Benchmarking
   c. Switching cost
   d. Strategic group

3. A _____ is any statistical hypothesis test in which the test statistic has a chi-square distribution when the null hypothesis is true, or any in which the probability distribution of the test statistic (assuming the null hypothesis is true) can be made to approximate a chi-square distribution as closely as desired by making the sample size large enough.

Some examples of chi-squared tests where the chi-square distribution is only approximately valid:

- Pearson's _____, also known as the chi-square goodness-of-fit test or _____ for independence. When mentioned without any modifiers or without other precluding context, this test is usually understood.
- Yates' _____, also known as Yates' correction for continuity.
- Mantel-Haenszel _____.
- Linear-by-linear association _____.
- The portmanteau test in time-series analysis, testing for the presence of autocorrelation
- Likelihood-ratio tests in general statistical modelling, for testing whether there is evidence of the need to move from a simple model to a more complicated one (where the simple model is nested within the complicated one.)

One case where the distribution of the test statistic is an exact chi-square distribution is the test that the variance of a normally-distributed population has a given value based on a sample variance. Such a test is uncommon in practice because values of variances to test against are seldom known exactly.

If a sample of size n is taken from a population having a normal distribution, then there is a well-known result which allows a test to be made of whether the variance of the population has a pre-determined value.

a. Type I error
b. Confounding variables
c. Randomization
d. Chi-square test

4. _____ is the identity of a group or culture, or of an individual as far as one is influenced by one's belonging to a group or culture. _____ is similar to and has overlaps with, but is not synonymous with, identity politics.

There are modern questions of culture that are transferred into questions of identity.

a. Power III
b. Cultural identity
c. 6-3-5 Brainwriting
d. 180SearchAssistant

5. _____ is a way of expressing knowledge or belief that an event will occur or has occurred. In mathematics the concept has been given an exact meaning in _____ theory, that is used extensively in such areas of study as mathematics, statistics, finance, gambling, science, and philosophy to draw conclusions about the likelihood of potential events and the underlying mechanics of complex systems.
a. Data
b. Heteroskedastic
c. Probability
d. Linear regression

6. '_____' is a class of statistical techniques that can be applied to data that exhibit 'natural' groupings. _____ sorts through the raw data and groups them into clusters. A cluster is a group of relatively homogeneous cases or observations.
a. Structure mining
b. Power III
c. 180SearchAssistant
d. Cluster analysis

7. In statistics, the _____, R^2 is used in the context of statistical models whose main purpose is the prediction of future outcomes on the basis of other related information. It is the proportion of variability in a data set that is accounted for by the statistical model. It provides a measure of how well future outcomes are likely to be predicted by the model.

a. Variance inflation factor
b. Coefficient of determination
c. Multicollinearity
d. Regression analysis

8. In grammar, the _____ is the form of an adjective or adverb which denotes the degree or grade by which a person, thing and is used in this context with a subordinating conjunction, such as than, as...as, etc.

The structure of a _____ in English consists normally of the positive form of the adjective or adverb, plus the suffix -er e.g. 'he is taller than his father is', or 'the village is less picturesque than the town nearby'.

a. Comparative
b. Power III
c. 180SearchAssistant
d. 6-3-5 Brainwriting

9. In the design of experiments, _____ are for studying the effects of one primary factor without the need to take other nuisance factors into account The experiment compares the values of a response variable based on the different levels of that primary factor.
a. Just-In-Case
b. Comprehensive,
c. Geo
d. Completely randomized designs

10. _____ is a statistical technique used in market research to determine how people value different features that make up an individual product or service.

The objective of _____ is to determine what combination of a limited number of attributes is most influential on respondent choice or decision making. A controlled set of potential products or services is shown to respondents and by analyzing how they make preferences between these products, the implicit valuation of the individual elements making up the product or service can be determined.

a. Semantic differential
b. Power III
c. Conjoint analysis
d. Likert scale

Chapter 19. The Research Report

11. In probability theory and statistics, _____ indicates the strength and direction of a linear relationship between two random variables. That is in contrast with the usage of the term in colloquial speech, denoting any relationship, not necessarily linear. In general statistical usage, _____ or co-relation refers to the departure of two random variables from independence.
   a. Frequency distribution
   b. Mean
   c. Probability
   d. Correlation

12. _____ refer to a collection of facts usually collected as the result of experience, observation or experiment or a set of premises. This may consist of numbers, words particularly as measurements or observations of a set of variables. _____ are often viewed as a lowest level of abstraction from which information and knowledge are derived.
   a. Sample size
   b. Mean
   c. Data
   d. Pearson product-moment correlation coefficient

13. _____ is a term used to describe a process of preparing and collecting data - for example as part of a process improvement or similar project.

_____ usually takes place early on in an improvement project, and is often formalised through a _____ Plan which often contains the following activity.

   1. Pre collection activity - Agree goals, target data, definitions, methods
   2. Collection - _____
   3. Present Findings - usually involves some form of sorting analysis and/or presentation.

A formal _____ process is necessary as it ensures that data gathered is both defined and accurate and that subsequent decisions based on arguments embodied in the findings are valid . The process provides both a baseline from which to measure from and in certain cases a target on what to improve. Types of _____ 1-By mail questionnaires 2-By personal interview

- Six sigma
- Sampling (statistics)

a. Power III
b. 180SearchAssistant
c. 6-3-5 Brainwriting
d. Data collection

14. _____ is a term for unprocessed data, it is also known as primary data. It is a relative term _____ can be input to a computer program or used in manual analysis procedures such as gathering statistics from a survey.
   a. Shoppers Food ' Pharmacy
   b. Product manager
   c. Chief marketing officer
   d. Raw data

15. In social science and psychometrics, _____ refers to whether a scale measures or correlates with a theorized psychological construct (such as 'fluid intelligence'.) It is related to the theoretical ideas behind the personality trait under consideration; a non-existent concept in the physical sense may be suggested as a method of organising how personality can be viewed. The unobservable idea of a unidimensional easier-to-harder dimension must be 'constructed' in the words of human language and graphics.
   a. Construct validity
   b. Criterion validity
   c. Predictive validity
   d. Discriminant validity

16. In psychometrics, _____ refers to the extent to which a measure represents all facets of a given social construct. For example, a depression scale may lack _____ if it only assesses the affective dimension of depression but fails to take into account the behavioral dimension. An element of subjectivity exists in relation to determining _____, which requires a degree of agreement about what a particular personality trait such as extraversion represents.
   a. Criterion validity
   b. Predictive validity
   c. Content validity
   d. Convergent validity

17. _____ is anything that is intended to save time, energy or frustration. A _____ store at a petrol station, for example, sells items that have nothing to do with gasoline/petrol, but it saves the consumer from having to go to a grocery store. '_____' is a very relative term and its meaning tends to change over time.

a. MaxDiff
b. Marketing buzz
c. Convenience
d. Demographic profile

18. In the absence of a more specific context, convergence denotes the approach toward a definite value, as time goes on; or to a definite point, a common view or opinion, or toward a fixed or equilibrium state. _____ is the adjectival form, and also a noun meaning an iterative approximation.

In mathematics, convergence describes limiting behaviour, particularly of an infinite sequence or series, toward some limit.

a. Convergent
b. Strict liability
c. Good things come to those who wait
d. Geo

19. _____ is the degree to which an operation is similar to (converges on) other operations that it theoretically should also be similar to. For instance, to show the _____ of a test of mathematics skills, the scores on the test can be correlated with scores on other tests that are also designed to measure basic mathematics ability. High correlations between the test scores would be evidence of a _____.
a. Criterion validity
b. Discriminant validity
c. Content validity
d. Convergent validity

20. _____ form a class of research methods that involve observation of some subset of a population of items all at the same time, in which, groups can be compared at different ages with respect of independent variables, such as IQ and memory. The fundamental difference between cross-sectional and longitudinal studies is that _____ take place at a single point in time and that a longitudinal study involves a series of measurements taken over a period of time. Both are a type of observational study.
a. 180SearchAssistant
b. Cross-sectional studies
c. Longitudinal studies
d. Power III

21. _____ describes data and characteristics about the population or phenomenon being studied. _____ answers the questions who, what, where, when and how.

Although the data description is factual, accurate and systematic, the research cannot describe what caused a situation.

a. Two-tailed test
b. Descriptive research
c. Power III
d. Sampling error

22. In algebra, the _____ of a polynomial with real or complex coefficients is a certain expression in the coefficients of the polynomial which is equal to zero if and only if the polynomial has a multiple root (i.e. a root with multiplicity greater than one) in the complex numbers. For example, the _____ of the quadratic polynomial

$$ax^2 + bx + c \text{ is } b^2 - 4ac.$$

The _____ of the cubic polynomial

$$ax^3 + bx^2 + cx + d \text{ is } b^2c^2 - 4ac^3 - 4b^3d - 27a^2d^2 + 18abcd.$$

a. Flighting
b. Consumption Map
c. Lifestyle center
d. Discriminant

23. Linear _____ and the related Fisher's linear discriminant are methods used in statistics and machine learning to find the linear combination of features which best separate two or more classes of objects or events. The resulting combination may be used as a linear classifier, or, more commonly, for dimensionality reduction before later classification.

LDiscriminant analysis is closely related to ANOVA (analysis of variance) and regression analysis, which also attempt to express one dependent variable as a linear combination of other features or measurements.

a. Multiple discriminant analysis
b. Linear discriminant analysis
c. Discriminant analysis
d. Geodemographic segmentation

24. _____ describes the degree to which the operationalization is not similar to (diverges from) other operationalizations that it theoretically should not be similar to.

Campbell and Fiske (1959) introduced the concept of _____ within their discussion on evaluating test validity. They stressed the importance of using both discriminant and convergent validation techniques when assessing new tests.

   a. Discriminant validity
   b. Predictive validity
   c. Convergent validity
   d. Criterion validity

25. In statistics, _____ is a collective name for techniques for the modeling and analysis of numerical data consisting of values of a dependent variable and of one or more independent variables The dependent variable in the regression equation is modeled as a function of the independent variables, corresponding parameters, and an error term. The error term is treated as a random variable.
   a. Regression analysis
   b. Variance inflation factor
   c. Stepwise regression
   d. Multicollinearity

26. _____ is one of the four elements of marketing mix. An organization or set of organizations (go-betweens) involved in the process of making a product or service available for use or consumption by a consumer or business user.

The other three parts of the marketing mix are product, pricing, and promotion.

   a. Distribution
   b. Japan Advertising Photographers' Association
   c. Better Living Through Chemistry
   d. Comparison-Shopping agent

27. A _____, in the field of business and marketing, is a geographic region or demographic group used to gauge the viability of a product or service in the mass market prior to a wide scale roll-out. The criteria used to judge the acceptability of a _____ region or group include:

   1. a population that is demographically similar to the proposed target market; and
   2. relative isolation from densely populated media markets so that advertising to the test audience can be efficient and economical.

The _____ ideally aims to duplicate 'everything' - promotion and distribution as well as `product' - on a smaller scale. The technique replicates, typically in one area, what is planned to occur in a national launch; and the results are very carefully monitored, so that they can be extrapolated to projected national results. The `area' may be any one of the following:

- Television area
- Test town
- Residential neighborhood
- Test site

A number of decisions have to be taken about any _____:

- Which _____?
- What is to be tested?
- How long a test?
- What are the success criteria?

The simple go or no-go decision, together with the related reduction of risk, is normally the main justification for the expense of _____s. At the same time, however, such _____s can be used to test specific elements of a new product's marketing mix; possibly the version of the product itself, the promotional message and media spend, the distribution channels and the price.

a. Test market
b. 180SearchAssistant
c. Preadolescence
d. Power III

28. A personal and cultural _____ is a relative ethic _____, an assumption upon which implementation can be extrapolated. A _____ system is a set of consistent _____s and measures that is soo not true. A principle _____ is a foundation upon which other _____s and measures of integrity are based.
a. Package-on-Package
b. Value
c. Perceptual maps
d. Supreme Court of the United States

29. _____ is a branch of philosophy which seeks to address questions about morality, such as how a moral outcome can be achieved in a specific situation (applied _____), how moral values should be determined (normative _____), what moral values people actually abide by (descriptive _____), what the fundamental semantic, ontological, and epistemic nature of _____ or morality is (meta-_____), and how moral capacity or moral agency develops and what its nature is (moral psychology.)

Socrates was one of the first Greek philosophers to encourage both scholars and the common citizen to turn their attention from the outside world to the condition of man. In this view, Knowledge having a bearing on human life was placed highest, all other knowledge being secondary.

   a. ADTECH
   b. AMAX
   c. ACNielsen
   d. Ethics

30. In probability theory and statistics, the _____ (or expectation value or mean and for continuous random variables with a density function it is the probability density -weighted integral of the possible values.

The term '_____' can be misleading.

   a. ACNielsen
   b. ADTECH
   c. AMAX
   d. Expected value

31. In decision theory, the _____ is the price that one would be willing to pay in order to gain access to perfect information.

The problem is modeled with a payoff matrix R_{ij} in which the row index i describes a choice that must be made by the payer, while the column index j describes a random variable that the payer does not yet have knowledge of, that has probability p_j of being in state j. If the payer is to choose i without knowing the value of j, the best choice is the one that maximizes the expected monetary value:

where

is the expected payoff for action i i.e. the expectation value, and is choosing the maximum of these expectations for all available actions.

a. AMAX
b. ACNielsen
c. ADTECH
d. Expected value of perfect information

32. _____ is a type of research conducted because a problem has not been clearly defined. _____ helps determine the best research design, data collection method and selection of subjects. Given its fundamental nature, _____ often concludes that a perceived problem does not actually exist.
a. ACNielsen
b. Intent scale translation
c. IDDEA
d. Exploratory research

33. In economics, an externality or spillover of an economic transaction is an impact on a party that is not directly involved in the transaction. In such a case, prices do not reflect the full costs or benefits in production or consumption of a product or service. A positive impact is called an _____ benefit, while a negative impact is called an _____ cost.
a. ACNielsen
b. AMAX
c. External
d. ADTECH

34. _____ is the validity of generalized (causal) inferences in scientific studies, usually based on experiments as experimental validity.

Inferences about cause-effect relationships based on a specific scientific study are said to possess _____ if they may be generalized from the unique and idiosyncratic settings, procedures and participants to other populations and conditions Causal inferences said to possess high degrees of _____ can reasonably be expected to apply (a) to the target population of the study (i.e. from which the sample was drawn) (also referred to as population validity), and (b) to the universe of other populations (e.g. across time and space.)

The most common loss of _____ comes from the fact that experiments using human participants often employ small samples obtained from a single geographic location or with idiosyncratic features (e.g. volunteers.)

a. AMAX
b. ACNielsen
c. External validity
d. ADTECH

35. _____ is a statistical method used to describe variability among observed variables in terms of fewer unobserved variables called factors. The observed variables are modeled as linear combinations of the factors, plus 'error' terms. The information gained about the interdependencies can be used later to reduce the set of variables in a dataset.
   a. Likert scale
   b. Semantic differential
   c. Power III
   d. Factor analysis

36. _____ is that part of statistical practice concerned with the selection of individual observations intended to yield some knowledge about a population of concern, especially for the purposes of statistical inference. Each observation measures one or more properties (weight, location, etc.) of an observable entity enumerated to distinguish objects or individuals.
   a. AStore
   b. Sports Marketing Group
   c. Richard Buckminster 'Bucky' Fuller
   d. Sampling

37. _____s are used in open sentences. For instance, in the formula x + 1 = 5, x is a _____ which represents an 'unknown' number. _____s are often represented by letters of the Roman alphabet, or those of other alphabets, such as Greek, and use other special symbols.
   a. Quantitative
   b. Book of business
   c. Personalization
   d. Variable

38. A _____ applies the scientific method to experimentally examine an intervention in the real world (or as many experimental economists like to say, naturally-occurring environments) rather than in the laboratory. _____s, like lab experiments, generally randomize subjects (or other sampling units) into treatment and control groups and compare outcomes between these groups. Clinical trials of pharmaceuticals are one example of _____s.

a. Power III
b. 180SearchAssistant
c. Response variable
d. Field experiment

39. A _____ is a form of qualitative research in which a group of people are asked about their attitude towards a product, service, concept, advertisement, idea, or packaging. Questions are asked in an interactive group setting where participants are free to talk with other group members.

Ernest Dichter originated the idea of having a 'group therapy' for products and this process is what became known as a _____.

a. Cross tabulation
b. Focus group
c. Logit analysis
d. Marketing research process

40. _____ includes the application or study of geodemographic classifications for business, social research and public policy but has a shorter history in academic research seeking to understand the processes by which settlements (notably, cities) evolve and neighborhoods are formed. It links the sciences of demography, the study of human population dynamics, geography, the study of the locational and spatial variation of both physical and human phenomena on Earth, and also sociology. In short, _____ is the science of profiling people based on where they live.
a. 6-3-5 Brainwriting
b. Power III
c. 180SearchAssistant
d. Geodemography

41. _____ is a metric or measure of business performance traditionally associated with sales. Defined as:

Sales can be measured either as the sum of dollars pursued or the number of deals pursued. Accurate calculation requires clear definition of when a sales opportunity is firm enough to be included in the metric, as well as firm disposition of the opportunity (i.e. the deal has reached a point where it is considered won, lost or abandoned.)

a. Sales management
b. Sales process
c. Lead generation
d. Hit rate

42. _____ is the validity of (causal) inferences in scientific studies, usually based on experiments as experimental validity .

Inferences are said to possess _____ if a causal relation between two variables is properly demonstrated . A causal inference may be based on a relation when three criteria are satisfied:

1. the 'cause' precedes the 'effect' in time (temporal precedence),
2. the 'cause' and the 'effect' are related (covariation), and
3. there are no plausible alternative explanations for the observed covariation (nonspuriousness) .

In scientific experimental settings, researchers often manipulate a variable (the independent variable) to see what effect it has on a second variable (the dependent variable) For example, a researcher might, for different experimental groups, manipulate the dosage of a particular drug between groups to see what effect it has on health. In this example, the researcher wants to make a causal inference, namely, that different doses of the drug may be held responsible for observed changes or differences.

a. ADTECH
b. ACNielsen
c. AMAX
d. Internal validity

43. In statistics, an _____ is a term in a statistical model added when the effect of two or more variables is not simply additive. Such a term reflects that the effect of one variable depends on the values of one or more other variables.

Thus, for a response Y and two variables x_1 and x_2 an additive model would be:

$$Y = ax_1 + bx_2 + \text{error}$$

In contrast to this,

$$Y = ax_1 + bx_2 + c(x_1 \times x_2) + \text{error},$$

is an example of a model with an _____ between variables x_1 and x_2 ('error' refers to the random variable whose value by which y differs from the expected value of y.)

a. AMAX
b. ACNielsen
c. ADTECH
d. Interaction

44. A _____ is a statement or claim that a particular event will occur in the future in more certain terms than a forecast. The etymology of this word is Latin . In regards to predicting the future Howard H. Stevenson Says, '_____ is at least two things: Important and hard.' Important, because we have to act, and hard because we have to realize the future we want, and what is the best way to get there.
   a. 180SearchAssistant
   b. Power III
   c. 6-3-5 Brainwriting
   d. Prediction

45. The _____ is a professional association for marketers. As of 2008 it had approximately 40,000 members. There are collegiate chapters on 250 campuses.
   a. ADTECH
   b. AMAX
   c. ACNielsen
   d. American Marketing Association

46. In common law systems that rely on testimony by witnesses, a _____ is a question that suggests the answer or contains the information the examiner is looking for. For example, this question is leading:

- You were at Duffy's bar on the night of July 15, weren't you?

It suggests that the witness was at Duffy's bar on the night in question. The same question in a non-leading form would be:

- Where were you on the night of July 15?

This form of question does not suggest to the witness the answer the examiner hopes to elicit.

_____s may often be answerable with a yes or no (though not all yes-no questions are leading), while non-_____s are open-ended. Depending on the circumstances _____s can be objectionable or proper.

a. Power III
b. Substantive law
c. Contract price
d. Leading question

47. _____ is defined by the American _____ Association as the activity, set of institutions, and processes for creating, communicating, delivering, and exchanging offerings that have value for customers, clients, partners, and society at large. The term developed from the original meaning which referred literally to going to market, as in shopping, or going to a market to sell goods or services.

_____ practice tends to be seen as a creative industry, which includes advertising, distribution and selling.

a. Marketing
b. Customer acquisition management
c. Product naming
d. Marketing myopia

48. Consumer market research is a form of applied sociology that concentrates on understanding the behaviours, whims and preferences, of consumers in a market-based economy, and aims to understand the effects and comparative success of marketing campaigns. The field of consumer _____ as a statistical science was pioneered by Arthur Nielsen with the founding of the ACNielsen Company in 1923.

Thus _____ is the systematic and objective identification, collection, analysis, and dissemination of information for the purpose of assisting management in decision making related to the identification and solution of problems and opportunities in marketing.

a. Marketing research
b. Logit analysis
c. Marketing research process
d. Focus group

49. A _____ is a research instrument consisting of a series of questions and other prompts for the purpose of gathering information from respondents. Although they are often designed for statistical analysis of the responses, this is not always the case. The _____ was invented by Sir Francis Galton.

a. Questionnaire
b. Market research
c. Mystery shopping
d. Mystery shoppers

Chapter 19. The Research Report

50. _____ is an advertisement in which a particular product specifically mentions a competitor by name for the express purpose of showing why the competitor is inferior to the product naming it.

This should not be confused with parody advertisements, where a fictional product is being advertised for the purpose of poking fun at the particular advertisement, nor should it be confused with the use of a coined brand name for the purpose of comparing the product without actually naming an actual competitor. ('Wikipedia tastes better and is less filling than the Encyclopedia Galactica.')

In the 1980s, during what has been referred to as the cola wars, soft-drink manufacturer Pepsi ran a series of advertisements where people, caught on hidden camera, in a blind taste test, chose Pepsi over rival Coca-Cola.

  a. Comparative advertising
  b. Cost per conversion
  c. Heavy-up
  d. GL-70

51. In probability theory and statistics, the _____ of a random variable, probability distribution, or sample is a measure of statistical dispersion, averaging the squared distance of its possible values from the expected value (mean.) Whereas the mean is a way to describe the location of a distribution, the _____ is a way to capture its scale or degree of being spread out. The unit of _____ is the square of the unit of the original variable.
  a. Standard deviation
  b. Correlation
  c. Variance
  d. Sample size

52. _____ is a statistical phenomenon in which two or more predictor variables in a multiple regression model are highly correlated. In this situation the coefficient estimates may change erratically in response to small changes in the model or the data. _____ does not reduce the predictive power or reliability of the model as a whole; it only affects calculations regarding individual predictors.
  a. Variance inflation factor
  b. Stepwise regression
  c. Regression analysis
  d. Multicollinearity

53. _____ is either an activity of a living being (such as a human), consisting of receiving knowledge of the outside world through the senses, or the recording of data using scientific instruments. The term may also refer to any datum collected during this activity.

The scientific method requires _____s of nature to formulate and test hypotheses.

a. ADTECH
b. ACNielsen
c. AMAX
d. Observation

54. Perceptual mapping is a graphics technique used by asset marketers that attempts to visually display the perceptions of customers or potential customers. Typically the position of a product, product line, brand, or company is displayed relative to their competition.

_____ can have any number of dimensions but the most common is two dimensions.

a. Retail floor planning
b. Developed country
c. Comparison-Shopping agent
d. Perceptual maps

55. A _____ is a tool used to measure the viewing habits of TV and cable audiences.

The _____ is a 'box', about the size of a paperback book. The box is hooked up to each television set and is accompanied by a remote control unit.

a. People meter
b. 6-3-5 Brainwriting
c. Power III
d. 180SearchAssistant

56. A sample is a subject chosen from a population for investigation. A _____ is one chosen by a method involving an unpredictable component. Random sampling can also refer to taking a number of independent observations from the same probability distribution, without involving any real population.
a. Selection bias
b. 180SearchAssistant
c. Random sample
d. Power III

57. In the field of marketing, demographics, opinion research, and social research in general, _____ variables are any attributes relating to personality, values, attitudes, interests, or lifestyles. They are also called IAO variables. They can be contrasted with demographic variables (such as age and gender), behavioral variables (such as usage rate or loyalty), and bizographic variables (such as industry, seniority and functional area.)

Chapter 19. The Research Report

a. Psychographic
b. Business-to-business
c. Marketing myopia
d. Lifetime value

58. _____s are errors in measurement that lead to measured values being inconsistent when repeated measures of a constant attribute or quantity are taken. The word random indicates that they are inherently unpredictable, and have null expected value, namely, they are scattered about the true value, and tend to have null arithmetic mean when a measurement is repeated several times with the same instrument. All measurements are prone to _____.
   a. Systematic error
   b. Power III
   c. 180SearchAssistant
   d. Random error

59. _____ is a sampling technique used when 'natural' groupings are evident in a statistical population. It is often used in marketing research. In this technique, the total population is divided into these groups (or clusters) and a sample of the groups is selected.
   a. Quota sampling
   b. Power III
   c. Cluster sampling
   d. Snowball sampling

60. In statistics, _____ is a method of sampling from a population.

When sub-populations vary considerably, it is advantageous to sample each subpopulation (stratum) independently. Stratification is the process of grouping members of the population into relatively homogeneous subgroups before sampling.

   a. Stratified sampling
   b. Data
   c. T-test
   d. Coefficient of variation

61. A number of different _____s are indicated below.

- Randomized controlled trial
    - Double-blind randomized trial
    - Single-blind randomized trial
    - Non-blind trial
- Nonrandomized trial (quasi-experiment)
    - Interrupted time series design (measures on a sample or a series of samples from the same population are obtained several times before and after a manipulated event or a naturally occurring event) - considered a type of quasi-experiment

- Cohort study
    - Prospective cohort
    - Retrospective cohort
    - Time series study
- Case-control study
    - Nested case-control study
- Cross-sectional study
    - Community survey (a type of cross-sectional study)

When choosing a _____, many factors must be taken into account. Different types of studies are subject to different types of bias. For example, recall bias is likely to occur in cross-sectional or case-control studies where subjects are asked to recall exposure to risk factors.

a. Power III
b. 180SearchAssistant
c. Longitudinal studies
d. Study design

62. _____ in survey research refers to the ratio of number of people who answered the survey divided by the number of people in the sample. It is usually expressed in the form of a percentage.

Example: if 1,000 surveys were sent by mail, and 257 were successfully completed and returned, then the _____ would be 25.7 %.

a. Reference value
b. Sentence completion tests
c. Power III
d. Response rate

Chapter 19. The Research Report

63. _____ is a form of Internet marketing that seeks to promote websites by increasing their visibility in search engine result pages (SERPs.) According to the _____ Professional Organization, _____ methods include: search engine optimization (or SEO), paid placement, contextual advertising, and paid inclusion. Other sources, including the New York Times, define _____ as the practice of buying paid search listings.
   a. Pay for placement
   b. Display advertising
   c. Blog marketing
   d. Search engine marketing

64. In statistics, _____ or estimation error is the error caused by observing a sample instead of the whole population.

An estimate of a quantity of interest, such as an average or percentage, will generally be subject to sample-to-sample variation. These variations in the possible sample values of a statistic can theoretically be expressed as _____s, although in practice the exact _____ is typically unknown.

   a. Two-tailed test
   b. Power III
   c. Varimax rotation
   d. Sampling error

65. Combining Existing _____ Sources with New Primary Data Sources

Imagine that we could get hold of a good collection of surveys taken in earlier years, such as detailed studies about changes going on in this phase and hopefully additional studies in the years to come. Analyzing this data base over time could give us a good picture of what changes actually have taken place in the orientation of the population and of the extent to which new technical concepts did have an impact on subgroups of the population. Furthermore, data archives can help to prepare studies on change over time by monitoring what questions have been asked in earlier years and alerting principal investigators to important questions which should be repeated in planned research projects.

   a. Power III
   b. Secondary data
   c. 6-3-5 Brainwriting
   d. 180SearchAssistant

66. _____ is a standard point of view or personal prejudice. especially when the tendency interferes with the ability to be impartial, unprejudiced, or objective. The term _____ed is used to describe an action, judgment, or other outcome influenced by a prejudged perspective.

a. 6-3-5 Brainwriting
b. Bias
c. Power III
d. 180SearchAssistant

67. In statistics, a _____ is an interval estimate of a population parameter. Instead of estimating the parameter by a single value, an interval likely to include the parameter is given. Thus, _____s are used to indicate the reliability of an estimate.
   a. Sample mean
   b. Linear regression
   c. T-test
   d. Confidence interval

68. _____ is the imitation of some real thing, state of affairs, or process. The act of simulating something generally entails representing certain key characteristics or behaviors of a selected physical or abstract system.

_____ is used in many contexts, including the modeling of natural systems or human systems in order to gain insight into their functioning.

   a. 180SearchAssistant
   b. Power III
   c. Simulation
   d. 6-3-5 Brainwriting

69. In statistics, a _____ is a mathematical relationship in which two occurrences have no causal connection, yet it may be inferred that they do, due to a certain third, unseen factor (referred to as a 'confounding factor' or 'lurking variable'.) The _____ gives an impression of a worthy link between two groups that is invalid when objectively examined.

The misleading correlation between two variables is produced through the operation of a third causal variable.

   a. 6-3-5 Brainwriting
   b. Power III
   c. 180SearchAssistant
   d. Spurious relationship

Chapter 19. The Research Report

70. _____ is the conveying of events in words, images, and sounds often by improvisation or embellishment. Stories or narratives have been shared in every culture and in every land as a means of entertainment, education, preservation of culture and in order to instill moral values. Crucial elements of stories and _____ include plot and characters, as well as the narrative point of view.
   a. Power III
   b. 6-3-5 Brainwriting
   c. 180SearchAssistant
   d. Storytelling

71. _____s are biases in measurement which lead to the situation where the mean of many separate measurements differs significantly from the actual value of the measured attribute. All measurements are prone to _____s, often of several different types. Sources of _____ may be imperfect calibration of measurement instruments, changes in the environment which interfere with the measurement process and sometimes imperfect methods of observation can be either zero error or percentage error.
   a. Power III
   b. Systematic error
   c. Systematic bias
   d. 180SearchAssistant

72. _____ is a statistical method involving the selection of elements from an ordered sampling frame. The most common form of _____ is an equal-probability method, in which every k^{th} element in the frame is selected, where k, the sampling interval (sometimes known as the 'skip'), is calculated as:

sample size (n) = population size (N) /k

Using this procedure each element in the population has a known and equal probability of selection. This makes _____ functionally similar to simple random sampling.

   a. Systematic sampling
   b. 180SearchAssistant
   c. Selection bias
   d. Power III

73. An _____ is a special-purpose computer system designed to perform one or a few dedicated functions, often with real-time computing constraints. It is usually embedded as part of a complete device including hardware and mechanical parts. In contrast, a general-purpose computer, such as a personal computer, can do many different tasks depending on programming.

a. Embedded system
b. ADTECH
c. ACNielsen
d. AMAX

74. _____ is the idea that the moral worth of an action is determined solely by its contribution to overall utility: that is, its contribution to happiness or pleasure as summed among all persons. It is thus a form of consequentialism, meaning that the moral worth of an action is determined by its outcome: put simply, the ends justify the means. Utility, the good to be maximized, has been defined by various thinkers as happiness or pleasure (versus suffering or pain), although preference utilitarians like Peter Singer define it as the satisfaction of preferences.
   a. Albert Einstein
   b. African Americans
   c. AStore
   d. Utilitarianism

75. _____ is a common word game involving an exchange of words that are associated together.

Once an original word has been chosen, usually randomly or arbitrarily, a player will find a word that they associate with it and make it known to all the players, usually by saying it aloud or writing it down as the next item on a list of words so far used. The next player must then do the same with this previous word.

   a. 180SearchAssistant
   b. 6-3-5 Brainwriting
   c. Power III
   d. Word association

ANSWER KEY

Chapter 1
1. d 2. d 3. d 4. b 5. d 6. b 7. b 8. c 9. c 10. b
11. d 12. a 13. a 14. c 15. a 16. c 17. a 18. d 19. d 20. b
21. a

Chapter 2
1. d 2. d 3. a 4. a 5. d 6. c 7. c 8. d 9. d 10. b
11. a 12. c 13. a 14. a 15. c 16. b 17. a

Chapter 3
1. d 2. b 3. d 4. b 5. a 6. c 7. b 8. d 9. d 10. d
11. c 12. c 13. a 14. c 15. d 16. b 17. d 18. d 19. d 20. d
21. b 22. a 23. d 24. a 25. a 26. b

Chapter 4
1. d 2. a 3. c 4. d 5. a 6. d 7. a 8. c 9. a 10. d
11. a 12. b 13. a 14. c 15. b 16. c 17. c 18. d 19. d

Chapter 5
1. d 2. d 3. b 4. d 5. a 6. c

Chapter 6
1. a 2. b 3. d 4. b 5. b 6. b 7. d 8. d 9. d 10. d
11. c 12. c 13. d 14. d 15. c 16. d 17. c 18. d 19. d 20. d
21. a 22. a 23. a 24. d 25. d 26. a 27. c 28. a

Chapter 7
1. b 2. d 3. d 4. d 5. d 6. a 7. d 8. a 9. d 10. d
11. c 12. d 13. a 14. d 15. c 16. d 17. a 18. a 19. a 20. b
21. d 22. c 23. d 24. a 25. c 26. d 27. d 28. c 29. d 30. d

Chapter 8
1. a 2. a 3. d 4. a 5. d 6. c 7. d 8. a 9. d 10. b
11. a 12. d 13. d 14. b 15. d 16. d 17. d 18. b 19. b 20. c
21. d 22. a 23. a 24. d

Chapter 9
1. a 2. d 3. d 4. d 5. d 6. d 7. c 8. d 9. b 10. d
11. d 12. d 13. d 14. b 15. c 16. c

Chapter 10
1. b 2. d 3. d 4. d 5. d 6. d 7. d 8. d 9. b 10. d
11. d 12. b 13. a 14. a 15. b 16. d 17. d 18. c 19. c 20. d
21. c 22. d

Chapter 11
| 1. c | 2. d | 3. d | 4. d | 5. c | 6. c | 7. d | 8. c | 9. d | 10. b |
| 11. a | 12. d | 13. d | 14. b | 15. d | 16. a | | | | |

Chapter 12
| 1. a | 2. a | 3. c | 4. a | 5. d | 6. d | 7. b | 8. d | 9. b | 10. d |

Chapter 13
| 1. d | 2. b | 3. c | 4. d | 5. d | 6. d | 7. a | 8. d | 9. d | 10. d |
| 11. d | 12. d | 13. d | 14. d | 15. b | 16. d | 17. a | | | |

Chapter 14
| 1. a | 2. d | 3. a | 4. b | 5. d | 6. a | 7. d | 8. c | 9. a | 10. c |
| 11. d | | | | | | | | | |

Chapter 15
| 1. a | 2. d | 3. d | 4. d | 5. d | 6. d | 7. d | 8. d | 9. c | 10. d |
| 11. c | | | | | | | | | |

Chapter 16
| 1. d | 2. a | 3. d | 4. d | 5. d | 6. a | 7. c | 8. d | 9. d | 10. d |

Chapter 17
| 1. d | 2. d | 3. a | 4. d | 5. c | 6. c | 7. d | 8. b | 9. d | 10. c |
| 11. a | 12. a | 13. c | 14. c | | | | | | |

Chapter 18
1. b	2. c	3. d	4. c	5. a	6. d	7. d	8. a	9. d	10. d
11. b	12. d	13. a	14. d	15. d	16. a	17. a	18. d	19. c	20. b
21. a	22. b	23. d	24. d						

Chapter 19
1. d	2. b	3. d	4. b	5. c	6. d	7. b	8. a	9. d	10. c
11. d	12. c	13. d	14. d	15. a	16. c	17. c	18. a	19. d	20. b
21. b	22. d	23. c	24. a	25. a	26. a	27. a	28. b	29. d	30. d
31. d	32. d	33. c	34. c	35. d	36. d	37. d	38. d	39. b	40. d
41. d	42. d	43. d	44. d	45. d	46. d	47. a	48. a	49. a	50. a
51. c	52. d	53. d	54. d	55. a	56. c	57. a	58. d	59. c	60. a
61. d	62. d	63. d	64. d	65. b	66. b	67. d	68. c	69. d	70. d
71. b	72. a	73. a	74. d	75. d					